P9-CLI-688

TLES

by Alan Lee

Written by David Day

Edited and Designed by David Larkin

 Bantam Books

Toronto   New York   London
Sydney   Auckland

An Original Bantam Gift Book
published in co-operation with
IAN AND BETTY BALLANTINE

CASTLES
October, 1984

All rights reserved.
Text copyright © 1984 by David Day.
Dust jacket and inside art copyright © 1984 by Alan Lee.
Project art directed and designed by
David Larkin, Becontree Press.
Text composition by Scorpion Pica.

The poem *The Ruin*
from *The Earliest English Poems*
© 1966, 1977 Michael Alexander
is printed by kind permission of Penguin Books, Ltd.

This book may not be reproduced in whole or in part,
by mimeograph or any other means, without
permission. For information, address: Bantam Books, Inc.

Library of Congress Catalogue Publication Data:
Lee, Alan.
  Castles.
  (An Original Bantam gift book)
  Bibliography: p. 192
  1. Castles—Europe—Folklore.
2. Castles in literature.
3. Legends—Europe. I. Day, David, 1947–
II. Larkin, David. III. Title.
GR135.L38   1984   398.2′094   84-45175
ISBN 0-553-05066-4

Published simultaneously in the United States and Canada

Bantam Books are published by Bantam Books, Inc. Its trade-
mark, consisting of the words 'Bantam Books' and the por-
trayal of a rooster, is Registered in the United States
Patent and Trademark Office and in other countries. Marca
Registrada. Bantam Books, Inc., 666 Fifth Avenue, New York,
New York, 10103.

PRINTED IN ITALY BY AMILCARE PIZZI

0 9 8 7 6 5 4 3 2 1

CONTENTS

12 Introduction

14 THE AGE OF MYTHS : Origins: Castles of the Gods:
Castles of Giants: Castles of the Faeries

72 THE AGE OF ROMANCE: King Arthur and Camelot:
The Court of Charlemagne: Siegfried and the Rhine Castles

137 THE AGE OF FANTASY: Castles in Fantastical Literature:
Castles in Fairy Tales: Castles in Modern Fantasy

192 Bibliography

The shattered wall,
the broken tower
have a story to tell –
from the touchstones of ruins
and ancient texts
we make a pilgrimage.

As we pass through a gate of dream, bright images arise, vibrant in the sunlight: the realms of old heroes spring to life from fragments of history and myth and tales of ancient wonders. In the clear eternal element of imagination a symphony of stone arches and marble chambers climb upward. These are the castles, dwelling-places of giants and gods, faeries and monsters, dwarfs and maidens, knights and sorcerers, kings and queens.

Here, in these thronging courtyards and great halls we are welcomed.

INTRODUCTION

CASTLE – an idea waiting to be born of rock. Look to the word itself, from the Latin *castrum*, a fort, and the old English *castel*, a stronghold. A hill fort, a palisaded dwelling-place, a citadel, a walled town. The parapets went up, the towers arose, the moat enclosed, the barbican guarded, the inner walls made safe the great keep that loomed over the realm.

The castle is the emblem of the civilization of western man. It is the manifestation of that culture's stern power and high romance. In certain respects, it may be said that all the history of Europe could be found within the boundary stones of her castles.

The castle implies order, the rule and enforcement of law and government. Stability, protection, limitation. The castle was the centre of mediaeval life, and it became the whole world in microcosm. It protected the seat of earthly power, the throne, it contained the symbol of heaven, the chapel, and it threatened with the symbol of hell, the dungeon.

The nature of the castle's enclosed world is determined by the master who shaped and commanded it. Outwardly it might be seen as a mandala or a maze: a saint's paradise or a demon's labyrinth. A place of peace and safety, or a hell on earth. In either case, and in forcing entrance or defending it, the castle became the symbol of spiritual strength. The forces of light or darkness, good or evil, life and death were implicit in the struggle.

That the castle in all its metaphoric implications was understood by all who lived in the great ages of castles cannot be doubted. The oldest surviving morality play (pre-dating even *Everyman*) is the *Castle of Perseverance*. It traces Man from the creation to the day of judgement, and views the journey as a battle between the Good Angel and the Bad Angel for the soul. In a world beset with evil and temptations the Good Angel protects the soul of Man by placing him in the Castle of Perseverance. Here, despite a siege army of the Deadly Sins and the Forces of Hell, Man is secure. The evil enemy, for all its might, cannot overwhelm the Castle. So long as he stays in it, he is safe, but if he is tempted to go out, he may face eternal damnation.

The meaning of the Castle is direct and unmistakable, and it is an allegory as much psychological as moral.

That was so then, as much as it was six centuries later in the twentieth century when Kafka took up the same allegory in his last novel, *The Castle* except that his view was from the outside looking in – one of the damned attempting to gain entrance *into* the Castle.

The Book of Castles takes the wanderer through three great ages of castle lore: the Age of Myth, the Age of Romance, and the Age of Fantasy.

The Age of Myth saw the creation of origins: tales of floating towers and subterranean kingdoms: the stories of Castles in the Air, the dwellings of the gods over the rainbow bridge: the castles of ice in the dark mountain realm of giants. And the castles of Faerie in lost kingdoms beneath the sea.

It is from this Age of Myth that the inspired builders of the castles of later ages come. The magician architects, the giants, the dwarfs, the sorceresses, the elves who possess the powers to bestow magical properties and cast spells about them. It is the Age of Myth which gives the castle its supernatural powers.

The Age of Romance properly begins with Arthur's Camelot – the Utopian age of the castle, where chivalry was born and all that was truly to do with romance had its origins. Camelot defined the ideal, but Arthurian Britain was filled with as many castles as there were human virtues and vices, desires and wishes. And the knights in this dream realm went in search of them all.

On the continent of Europe, the Holy Roman Emperor Charlemagne stood at the centre of all tales of romance. Like Arthur in Camelot, Charlemagne at Aix-la-Chapelle formed a mighty alliance of knights, his Palladins, who, in the common cause of Christianity, achieved great deeds. The great heroes of Europe gained fame by crushing pagan and Moorish threats to their Christian realms. They stormed and destroyed heathen strongholds, and maintained their own dominance from their castles: Ogier the Dane in Elsinore Castle, Siegfried in Xanten on the Rhine, Etzel in Castle Gran in Hungary on the Danube, Dietrich from his palace in Verona.

The Age of Fantasy begins with a roar and a puff of smoke. It begins when gunpowder and cannonball began to destroy the physical existence of castles as thoroughly as the old gods might have had they loosed their thunderbolts.

The Age of Fantasy is a flight to castles of pure imagination in an age of literate story-tellers who composed with a pen. This age saw wonderful tales come to life, and heroes to match them – Orlando, Amadis of Gaul, Huon of Bordeaux, and many more.

The ancient vision of castles is guarded most jealously in the world of folklore and fairy tale where old legends and beliefs have been transformed into castles for a Sleeping Beauty, or a Blue Beard, Jack-the-Giant-Killer or Beauty and the Beast.

Until at last we come to the castles of a time more familiar but no less wondrous – from the beginnings of the Gothic romances of Walpole and Scott through to the strange creations of Poe, Stoker, Tolkien and Peake. All draw on the traditions and legends of the past, yet each has added something new, individual, reinventing the wonder of castles for our own age. The shimmer of distant magic lights the horizons of the human mind, at once a haunting memory and a beckoning promise 🏰

THE AGE OF MYTHS

ORIGINS

BEFORE 'CASTLE' WAS EVEN A WORD, a great invasion of barbarians swept over the continent of Europe. These were the Norse and Teutonic tribes who found themselves suddenly masters in the midst of the ruins of lost civilizations.

Upon the lonely windswept hilltops were the stone remains of prehistoric forts where men once fought with flint axes. There were the rounded mounds of old Celtic Caers, the crumbling remains of forts and towers of the bronze and iron ages. Still standing were the Roman 'castrum' forts and the 'castellum' watchtowers rising upon rocky promontories. These were the stone walls of castels, abandoned garrisons of legions long vanished.

Elsewhere were massive, impossibly huge circles of monolithic stones standing on broad plains, and vast burial mounds, the barrow graves of forgotten kings. The lands were crisscrossed with the lines of ancient power, dragon-roads made by Druid wizard-priests; and by wide Roman roads, and canals. Then there were huge earthworks and the gigantic images of men and beasts cut into the mountainsides.

The waves of invaders were as fascinated by the ruins as the men of centuries later. Among the oldest fragments of the written literature of the Teutonic tribes are lines by one who thought deeply on the old stones his people found:

'Well-wrought this wall: Wierds broke it.
The stronghold burst . . .
Snapped rooftrees, towers fallen,
the work of Giants, the stonesmiths,
mouldereth.

        Rime scoureth gatetowers
          rime on mortar
Shattered the showershields, roofs ruined,
age underate them.

        And the wielders and wrights?
Earthgrip holds them – gone, long gone,
fast in gravesgrasp while fifty fathers
and sons have passed.'

And with the meditation on fallen power, he thought, too,
of the life that was once within:

   'There once many a man
mood-glad, goldbright, of gleams garnished,
flushed with wine-pride, flashing war-gear,
gazed on wrought gemstones, on gold, on silver,
on wealth held and hoarded, on light-filled amber,
on this bright burg of broad dominion.'

Looking at the towers in the mist, the usurpers could only imagine they were built by magic. For though the Norsemen and the Teutons were fine master-builders in wood and were skilled metal workers, the wizardry of massive stonework was beyond their abilities.

In their way, they were not wrong about the architects. Many centuries before even the Romans, with their high engineering skills, marched north, there must have been an ancient priesthood, of workers of magic, who were, at the very least, consummate builders. They were the creators of many massive stone monuments – the observatory-temple of Stonehenge among them.

19

THE IDEA OF THE MAGICIAN-ARCHITECT was an ancient one, deeply connected to the belief that in all such great ventures a bargain must always be struck with the Earth-Spirits. When a building or monument is raised, a magician must at least be consulted about the nature of the Earth-Spirits who might disturb the foundations or plague the structure.

There is one tale about that most famous of magicians, the great enchanter Merlin, that brings to light the need to appease or control the Earth-Spirits. The Merlin of this tale, however, is very much in the ancient traditions of the Druids that far pre-date the era of Camelot. It is a tradition that makes him a dark prophet, a demon-child who spoke at birth, a creature more faerie than human.

THE CASTLE AND THE DRAGONS

HEN THE TRAITOR AND USURPER called Vortigern declared himself King of Britain he ordered the building of a vast castle to be the centre of his kingdom.

Work on the castle went on at a great rate, but to no avail, for the walls, no matter how thick and solid, would not stand. Each day the walls were built, and each night they collapsed in a heap.

The king's astrologers and necromancers claimed there must be a blood sacrifice so that the curse on the castle would be raised. They declared that the king must find a child with no earthly father and have him slain on the castle site.

Now it was known that there was a child called Merlin, born of a demon and a virgin. But when King Vortigern had this child brought before him he was so impressed by Merlin's prophetic skills that he thought it prudent to ask the child merely to tell him the cause of the falling walls.

Merlin immediately told the king that if he dug a deep pit in the earth beneath what would be the throne room, he would soon discover the source of the turmoil.

The king at once ordered that this be done. He was astonished when his workers uncovered two great dragons, one red and one white, entwining in an eternal conflict that literally shook the earth. Once the pit was opened, however, the huge reptiles rose up out of the ground and continued their monstrous battle all about the countryside. At last the white dragon killed the red, then flew up and vanished from sight.

Grateful that now he might safely build his castle, the king asked the child of power if the dragons were an omen of things to come. Merlin replied that they were, and moreover, that the king, like the dragon, would soon be killed in a fiery conflict and the walls of his castle laid low and for the last time.

The prophecy proved true, for another powerful warlord came to challenge Vortigern's claim to the throne. Vortigern fled to his castle, but his rival pursued him and put the castle to the torch. There amid the flames and collapsing walls, Vortigern came to a fiery end.

WHEN THE NORSEMEN AND TEUTONS came to build their own settlements and their huge, splendid feasting halls, they often chose the ancient sites of the ruined Ring Forts.

Sometimes they might build on what had once been the consecrated ground of forgotten gods, or even unknown graves. And many are the tales of curses visited on those who offended the spirits of the dead. For what had once been sacred groves were now neglected, becoming dark forests and swamps that bred nightmare tales of avenging spirits, monsters, demons and even dragons to haunt the usurpers in the darkness of night.

THE TALE OF THE CURSE of an evil spirit visited on the splendid
gold-roofed Victory Hall of Hrothgar, King of Denmark, is the central story
of that first epic of the northern peoples, the poem *Beowulf*. It is a tale that
vividly provides the archetypes for the legends of the haunted castles of later
times.

HEOROT — THE HAUNTED HALL

O F ALL THE GREAT HALLS that stood in the world, it is claimed that none could match the splendour of Heorot the Golden. This was the Hall of Victory that King Hrothgar of Denmark built on the high citadel of his kingdom's stronghold.

From the beginning Heorot was ill-fated. On its inauguration day, in the midst of the first night of feasting, there came to the high horn-gabled hall a vengeful cannibal spirit called Grendel. After warriors and guests had drunk their fill, Grendel came on them in their sleep and viciously murdered them.

Heorot the Golden became a bloody charnel house. Each night any who dared remain within were slain and devoured by the monster. Beyond his terrible strength, Grendel was protected by a sorcerous spell that allowed no weapon to pierce his hide. For twelve long years the monstrous Grendel haunted Heorot by night.

By day the bloodthirsty monster lived in a foul mere, deep and stagnant, in the heart of the black-dark forest. There, under the filthy water, together with his Ogress mother – an even more vile creature – he dwelled in a hellish fire-glimmering Great Hall. The Hall was alive with great serpents and misshapen creatures of all kinds, and there, too, were hordes of gold and jewelled weapons stolen from slain heroes and looted graves.

At last the hero Beowulf came to Denmark, and Hrothgar received him with high ceremony and a fine banquet. And when Beowulf made it clear that he intended to fight Grendel, Hrothgar tried to dissuade him. But as night came on, Beowulf and his companions calmly laid themselves down in the cursed Hall, while all others left.

In the dead of night, Grendel came. With a single wrench he tore the door – iron bars, bolts and all – from its frame and entered the Hall. Swiftly he seized a sleeping warrior, ripped the man's head from his shoulders, drank the fountain of blood and ate the raw flesh.

Next Grendel reached out in the dark for Beowulf. But the hero knew that iron weapons would not harm the creature, and with a vice-like grip he seized the monster by the arm.

28

BURNING WITH PAIN and anger, Grendel in turn attacked Beowulf. But the beast had never encountered such strength. The Hall rocked and shook with their wrestling. At last Beowulf wrenched the arm of the beast clear out of its shoulder. Howling with pain from this fatal wound, Grendel fled to his lair and there died in agony.

Joyful at their release from the tyranny of the monster, the Danes took the gory trophy of the creature's torn limb with its clawlike hand and hung it from a high rafter in the Hall of Heorot.

But their celebration was short-lived. That very night there came to the Hall another monstrous being – the vicious Ogress, come to retrieve her son's torn limb, and to exact a bloody revenge.

Once again Beowulf came to do battle, but this time he descended into the very mere itself. Beneath the foul waters he dared to enter the fiery hall of the Ogress. There, in a vicious battle and using a charmed sword, he cut the fiend's head from her body. The whole pool was set to boiling with her hot and evil blood.

At last the curse of Heorot was raised. Hrothgar once again became master in his own kingdom, and the hero Beowulf was rewarded with golden gifts and immortal fame.

EVEN IN BEOWULF'S TIME, there was one Great Hall which, though it might be less gilded or splendid than Heorot, was certainly more famous and honoured. This was the Hall called Branstock that was built by the Swedish King Volsung – and to whose door came a strange visitor.

BRANSTOCK –
THE HALL OF THE VOLSUNGS

THE DYNASTIC HOUSE of King Volsung was raised around a huge, sacred oak that was called Branstock, and as this tree was the central pillar of the structure, the Great Hall itself came to be known by this name.

To Volsung's Hall came many a traveller and lord, nor indeed was any man turned away from this most hospitable Great Hall. But one night late, there came an old, one-eyed visitor, seeking shelter from a bitter storm.

Although many of the assembled guests did not much like the wily appearance of the silent old man, Volsung, with due respect for his age, treated him courteously and well. After a time, when the traveller had eaten and drunk his fill, he stood up, opened his cape, and revealed a marvellous, glittering sword. The guests drew back in alarm, but the old man turned from them and, with supernatural strength, thrust the blade hilt-deep into the great oak.

Then, to the guests and king, the old man, his single wizard's eye glinting, declared that here was a weapon that was to be the gift of gods to the warrior who could draw it from its wooden sheath. He then walked out of the Hall and vanished into the night.

There were none in the Hall who doubted that the old man was Odin the All-Father, the one-eyed King of the Gods, known to travel the world in the guise of an old wizard and work many feats of wonder.

The god-given gift sword was the dream of every great warrior, so all the men in the Hall vied for a chance to win it. But none could draw it from the tree. Of Volsung's own ten strong sons, the nine elder had all tried, and the tenth did not believe he could succeed where the others had failed. Finally, as all others had tried, Sigmund, the youngest Volsung, at last placed his hand on the hilt. To his total amazement the sword slipped out of the tree and into his hand with perfect ease.

Sigmund the Volsung was Odin's chosen champion, and with that great blade, Sigmund and all his heirs were to win fame greater than any mortal before them.

THE TALE OF BRANSTOCK chronicles a major theme in arcane lore – that of the hero mysteriously gifted by god or wizard with a weapon having magical powers. It is a motif that most obviously precedes the tale of Merlin and the sword in the stone, but the idea appears in many forms, the magic gift suitably transmuted to meet the particular threat.

IN THE VOLSUNG SAGA, the eventual inheritor of Odin's sword is Sigmund's son, the famous Sigurd the Dragonslayer. This sword becomes the link to another magical motif, for among Sigurd's many exploits is an adventure that is the model for all tales of enchanted princesses held under a spell of sleep – a spell also cast by Odin! So the God's magic sword comes full circle . . .

THE VALKYRIE'S TOWER

ONCE, AMONG THE VALKYRIES, the immortal warrior-maidens of the Gods, there was one named Brynhild who was wilful and not obedient to the great Odin. In wrath Odin cast her out of the kingdom of the gods.

On the barren mountain Hindfell he erected a stone tower ringed with a wall of giant shields and a moat of eternal flame, and within the tower he placed the beautiful battle-maiden in a deep trance from the magical thorn of sleep that Odin had pressed to her breast.

There, on the fiery mountain in the Tower of the Valkyrie, Brynhild the sleeping beauty lay enchanted for many years. Finally, the young Dragonslayer, Sigurd the Volsung, learning of the Tower, came to the rescue of the maid. Fearlessly he braved the moat of fire and rode through the flames. Then he took the sword of Odin and sheared a wide door through the wall of shields built by Odin.

So Sigurd was able to enter the tower and found the lovely Brynhild in a deep sleep. He took from her the battle-maiden's armour and discovered the thorn, which he withdrew. Immediately the enchantment was broken and Brynhild awoke to greet her rescuer.

THE QUEST for an earthly paradise is a theme that occurs throughout all time, in all lands. Among the later tales of the Vikings is that of two heroes who search for a magical realm called Odainsaker, the Glittering Pláin.

THE CASTLE IN THE AIR

THE TWO HEROES, Erik of Denmark and Erik of Norway, once set out to discover the realm of Odainsaker, said to be in a land east of India. They travelled far and long, and at length came to a river crossed by a stone bridge. On the far side stood a ravenous dragon waiting to devour any who ventured over. Erik of Denmark hesitated, but Erik of Norway, like a mad berserker, rushed into the gaping jaws of the dragon and was immediately consumed in a burst of flame.

Mourning the loss of his companion, Erik of Denmark went home. But after the passage of many years, the lost Erik reappeared in Norway. The dragon had been an illusion, and proved indeed to be a gateway to a wonderful plain, gleaming with star-like flowers of heavenly perfumes. It was a land of eternal summer where no creature even cast a shadow. There Erik of Norway travelled until he found a delicate tower suspended in mid-air. A ladder hung down, so the hero climbed up.

In the tower was everything he could wish for – fine food, rich wine, luxurious furnishings – and a perfume that filled him with constant joy. He was sure he had found Odainsaker, the Glittering Plain.

In time, however, it was revealed that this place was but a drab imitation of the real Odainsaker, and if he wished to go on to the true Paradise, he must understand that it was a land of no return. Faced with this critical choice, Erik of Norway decided he would not go on, but for a time at least would return to the world of his companions and kinsmen.

CASTLES OF GODS AND GIANTS

OUT OF THEIR CONTEMPLATION of massive stonework ruins, out of tales of lost paradise, out of pure imagination, the Norsemen built their own vision of heaven and hell. But the scale of their vision was far beyond that of Erik of Norway's floating tower.

The approach to the dwelling-place of their Gods was guarded by Heimdall's Hall on the greatest drawbridge ever imagined – Bifrost, the Rainbow Bridge that arched over the whole sky. This was the gigantic causeway over which the Gods rode to the gates of their castle in the air – Asgard, the walled citadel that held the huge halls and towers of their realm.

ASGARD

THE TALLEST TOWER IN ASGARD was Hlidskiaff, the watchtower, where Odin, King of the Gods, often sat on his golden throne, shadowed only by the topmost branches of Yggdrasil, the world tree. From the watchtower Odin could survey all the lands of the Nine Worlds. Not just Asgard, the realm of the Gods, or Midgard (Middle-earth), where those mortal beings called Men lived, but also Alheim and Swarthalheim, the lands of the Light and Dark Elves – and other worlds, of Vanaheim, home of the brilliant Vanir, spirits of the high air, and the dark regions of caverns and mist beneath the earth called Nifelheim where the Dwarfs worked their mines.

There were the huge northern realms of mountains and ice called Jotunheim and Utgard where the Frost and Mountain Giants made their home. To the south was Muspellsheim, 'the Land of Fire', where the Fire Giants dwelt. The deepest world of all was the terrible land of Hel, where the dead walked in eternal darkness and Garm the giant Hound of Hel guarded the gate.

In the highest kingdom of Asgard each god possessed a great hall in the citadel, but Odin the All-Father commanded three. The first was Valaskiaff, 'Heaven's Crag', where the watchtower Hlidskiaff stood. Odin's second hall was Gladsheim. This was the council hall of the Gods where Odin presided over a circular table around which the twelve gods sat, each on a golden throne.

Most famous of all Odin's halls was Valhalla, the 'Hall of the Slain', the golden hall of warriors. Valhalla had five hundred and forty doors, each wide enough for eight hundred warriors to enter marching abreast. The walls were built with the glittering spears of giants, the roof was fashioned of shields of polished gold.

At the Hall's long tables, all heroic warriors who fell in battle were resurrected, and there they feasted and drank in the company of Odin, Lord of Victories. These warriors were 'the chosen slain' selected by the winged Valkyries from the heroic dead of Midgard. On their magical steeds they rode through the air high over Bifrost, carrying the brave dead to the very gates of Asgard and finally into Valhalla itself.

In that great hall, served by beautiful maidens and entertained by skalds, the heroes drank the mead and ate the boar's meat of the Gods. Then, having had their fill, the warriors would spring from their tables and challenge one another to deadly combat. The battles would be fought to the death, so that they might accomplish once again the feats of skill and daring by which they had won so much fame in Midgard.

The terrible destruction of each day's battle was ended with the blast of a great horn. Then all those slain or maimed would rise up, entirely healed and whole again, and return to the serious business of feasting and celebration.

THE VAST CITADEL OF ASGARD was not the only castle kingdom of the immortals. Indeed there were wondrous castles in all the realms of the Nine Worlds.

However, none surpassed those of the great malevolent earth-spirits, the Giants of the mountainous realms of Ice and Fire. These huge beings were also gifted with many sorcerous powers and were the real master architects of the Nine Worlds. In the building of castles, none could surpass them.

THE WALLS OF ASGARD

HEN IT CAME TO THE BUILDING of the walls of Asgard, even the Gods realized that none of them was capable of such a monumental task. Consequently they were forced to make a bargain with the only being in the Nine Worlds who could accomplish the deed. This was an evil Magician-Giant called Hrim-thurs.

The gods believed they would never have to make payment for the construction, as they had placed a time limit of one year for the work, an impossibility even for the huge Giant Architect. However, the Gods had reckoned without the giant's horse, Svadilfare. The magical beast worked at the command of his master so rapidly that it was clear the Giant would achieve his task in the time allotted.

This the Gods could not permit, for payment would have cost them the light of the sun and the moon, as well as the elixir by which they maintained their immortality. So it fell to the Trickster God, Loki, to cheat the Giant by the theft of his magnificent horse. Loki transformed himself into a mare and lured Svadilfare away. The offspring of this supernatural union was Sleipnir, the eight-footed horse of Odin. When the wrathful Giant pursued the Gods seeking reparation, the great God of Thunder, Thor, raised his thunderbolt hammer   and slew the huge being.

THIS WAS THE START
of a great war between the Gods
and the Giants. And because the
Gods had cheated the Giants,
it seemed that a curse was laid on
their kingdom. In the end, the Giants
had their revenge, for in a last great
conflict the walls of Asgard fell.
Yet, in their vast destruction,
all else in the Nine Worlds
was also destroyed.
This was the universal
holocaust, Ragnarok –
the twilight of
the Gods.

JOTUNHEIM – LAND OF THE GIANTS

THE LAND OF THE GIANTS, Jotunheim, was a desolate wasteland in the north. It was separated from the world of men by a bulwark of high mountains and the wide river Glivagar. It was a land of snow, ice and bone-chilling mists from which the monstrous and brutish Frost Giants issued forth on sporadic attacks upon the lands of Men. Here the Giants built many huge castles among the mountains and ice. Here they plotted their vengeful war against the Gods.

THE ICE CASTLE OF UTGARD-LOKE

ONCE THE GOD OF THUNDER, THOR, set out on an adventure into Jotunheim because the Frost Giants had been sending cold winds and killing frosts which had withered and blighted the crops of their neighbours. With his two companions, Loki and Thialfi, Thor sought out the Castle of Utgard-Loke, the King of the Frost Giants.

After a long and extremely difficult journey they came to a castle so immense that mighty Thor had to crane his neck to see its ramparts. It was built of great blocks of ice and towering icicles that served as pillars. The scale of the castle was so large that the Gods could enter easily by slipping through the grill-work of its huge gate.

Once within, the Gods presented themselves to the assembled Frost Giants who made fun of the diminutive size of the guests and poured scorn on the idea of their great powers. Soon it was proposed that the Gods should undergo a series of contests with the Giants in order that each might gauge the strength of the other.

Loki the Trickster held an eating contest with the Giant Loge, and although they finished their huge troughs of meat at the same time, Loge had consumed meat, bones and wooden trough as well – and hence was judged the winner.

Next the swift Thialfi was challenged to a footrace by a strange Dwarf called Huge, but in each of three races the God suffered humiliating defeat.

Thor the Thunderer was now challenged to three contests. The first was a drinking trial in which he attempted, with three huge draughts, to empty the Giant King's wineflask. Despite Thor's huge thirst he managed to reduce the contents of the horn by only the smallest margin.

Next Thor was mirthfully asked if he was capable of lifting the King's pet cat off the ground. Thor's tremendous strength was legendary, but when he tried to lift the resting cat, after the most terrific struggle all he could manage was to raise one paw off the ground.

Finally, amid the derision and laughter of the Frost Giants, the King said he would not ask Thor to test his strength against the strongest of the giants, for that would not even be a contest. Instead he sent out for his ancient Nurse, a weak old Giantess. Much put out, Thor wrestled furiously, only to find the old Nurse could handle him as though he were a baby.

The next day the shame-faced Gods left the Ice Castle totally dispirited by their failure. However, beyond the great gates they learned that they had been defeated by magic rather than by strength. Within the Castle of Ice, Utgard-Loke commanded great enchantments. The Giant Loge, who had eaten more than Loki the Trickster, was in fact Fire, which can consume everything, and the Dwarf Huge, who defeated Thialfi, was actually Thought, whom none can outrun.

The wine in the King's drinking vessel was really the Ocean, and though Thor failed to swallow it, he had succeeded in lowering its level. Similarly, the cat he had tried to lift was actually the Midgard Serpent, whose coils encircle the entire world, and the Old Nurse was really Old Age – whom no one, in the end, can defeat.

Furious at having been tricked and humiliated, Thor swore to have his revenge, whereupon, before his very eyes, the gigantic Ice Castle vanished into a mist leaving only the echoing laughter of the Frost Giants' scorn.

JOTUNHEIM was not the only land where Giant Magicians built their castles and kingdoms. In a journey that was as much a vision of Hell as Erik of Norway's voyage was a vision of Paradise, the Danish hero Thorkill set out for the Land of the Not-Dead.

THE CITY OF THE NOT-DEAD

THE ADVENTURER THORKILL was the hero chosen by the King of Denmark to lead an expedition of three hundred warriors into the strange and distant Land of the Not-Dead, a dreaded place of mists and phantoms and monsters.

When Thorkill and his men came within sight of the City it had the appearance of being insubstantial, made of evil vapours. Yet it proved to be as perilous as it was dismal. At its gates were ferocious hell-hounds, while the battlements, decorated with severed heads mounted on spikes, were unscalable.

Yet with great courage Thorkill and his band managed to gain entry and gradually worked their way through strange streets in which monstrous wraiths and undead spirits wandered, caught in this Limbo land of phantoms. Choking on the stench of corruption and death, the adventurers pushed on until at last they came to the mountainous ruin of a dwelling that was the fortress of the Slain King.

The King of this place was the Giant Geirrod who, long before, had plotted to kill the God Thor. Instead, Thor had seized the Giant's fiery javelin and thrown it with such force that it passed right through Geirrod and sank deep into the stone wall behind him. Yet, dead though he was, like some impaled vampire spirit he continued to be King in this place.

Thorkill led his men through Geirrod's fortress and the Halls of Torture where monsters guarded each door and the floors writhed with venomous snakes. They found Giants in the most grotesque postures of torturous death, stretched on benches of iron and looking as if they were carved in stone. Others moaned and squirmed, perpetually reliving their separate agonies.

At last they came to the Giant King Geirrod seated upon a ledge, his body still transfixed and held up by the javelin Thor had thrown. Beyond where the Slain King was impaled, Thorkill could see his goal. This was the Chamber of Treasures, a place filled with jewels and gold and all manner of beautiful weapons. Here he led his men, for here he would find the object of the quest, the King's Mantle. This was a king's robe, ablaze with jewels and radiant with silver and gold. It had a waistbelt and headgear of gold and gemstones and was furred with ermine.

The moment Thorkill seized the Mantle, the whole kingdom shook as if struck by an earthquake. Alarms and screams arose all about them, and all the beings that appeared to be dead sprang up to attack them. The castle itself seemed to shake with rage and hordes of phantoms and furies joined the fray to destroy the adventurers.

Such was the might of the curse on those who looted the kingdom of the Not-Dead, that of the three hundred who set out on the quest, only twenty returned.

CASTLES OF FAERIE

FROM THE TWILIGHT WORLD of faerie come the myths of the ancient Giants and Gods of the Celtic people and their own tales of castles. Most often the Castles of Faerie were hidden away from the eyes of mortals, on distant isles, inside hollow hills or even at the bottom of lakes and seas.

THE CASTLE OF BALOR

THE GREATEST BUILDER of ancient Ireland was one named Gobhan the Architect. He was the first builder of Round Towers, and through his skills as a magician and a smith, he was well known as a wonderful innovator and a builder of unique castles.

Now it happened that Gobhan was once commissioned to build a castle by a king of a race of deformed Giants, called the Fomors. This king, Balor of the Mighty Blows, knew that the Fomors had once ruled with an iron hand in Donegal, by virtue of their control of a magical tower of glass on Tory Island. Balor now wished to seize even greater power by having Gobhan build the largest castle with the tallest tower in all Ireland.

This the master-builder Gobhan did, but of course the Giant King Balor decided he could never allow Gobhan to leave his kingdom alive, for fear that he would go and build an even more splendid structure for someone else.

So just as Gobhan was completing the great tower, King Balor ordered the scaffolding taken away from under the Architect. Gobhan found himself stranded high up on the roof. Here the King intended to leave the builder until he died of starvation. However, Gobhan was no man's fool, and decided that anything he could make, he could also unmake. He at once started to descend by demolishing the tower, from the top down.

King Balor soon realized that all his plans for his kingdom would come to nothing if Gobhan were allowed to continue. Quickly he ordered the scaffolding and ladders returned.

A new bargain was then struck between the King and Gobhan. Repairs were made and Gobhan the Architect received his payment and his free passage out of the kingdom.

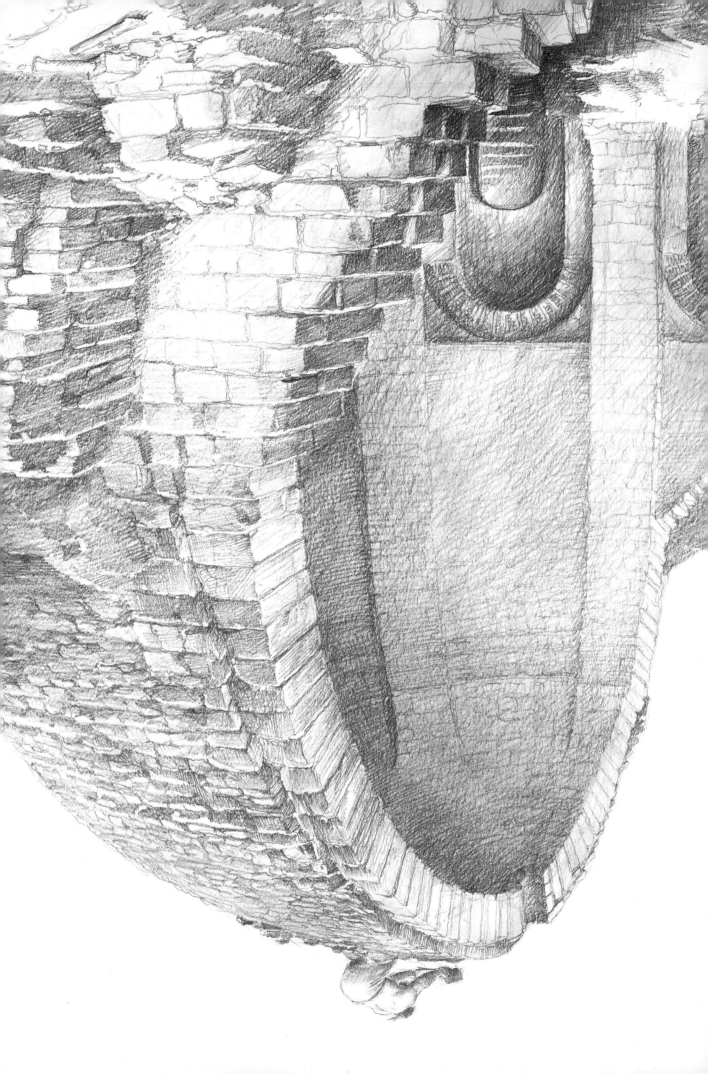

AMONG THE ANCIENT RACE of the Irish Gods – the Tuatha De Danaan – was one called the Dagda who became their King. The Dagda was a great warrior, a musician and a magician, but above all he was the Giant God of the Earth. It was he who with his huge strength built the Hollow Hills of Faerie.

For each of the Gods, the Dagda built a subterranean court that appeared to be a simple hill or riverbank, but which glittered within with wonders.

AMONG THE STRANGEST OF CASTLES ever made was that of the
Welsh sea god, Manawyddan the Wise. By his skills as a magician,
Manawyddan shaped a gruesome castle entirely out of human bones. This
was a prison castle for those who trespassed in his dark kingdom of Gower.
In fact it was a vast labyrinth divided into numberless prison chambers and
shaped like a huge beehive. There is one eccentric account of an early and
long-standing war between one tribe of Celts and the Romans that is evidently
based on the Sea God's Bone Castle.

THE CASTLE OF SKULLS

IN THAT TIME THE CELTS fought a great battle against the
Romans, slaying them by the thousand. Then the wild tribesmen
went down into the battlefield and gathered up all the skulls and
bones of slain Roman soldiers. Out of these the wily Celts built a
ghastly castle of skulls and bones in which they held all their prisoners-of-war.

The effect on the Romans was successfully unnerving. Horrified and
angered they returned, full of vengeance, and destroyed the Castle of Skulls.
But each time the Romans demolished it, the grisly Castle was rebuilt, larger
and stronger than before.

QUEST TO THE CASTLE
OF THE CAULDRON

THE THEME IMPLICIT in the constant renewal of the Castle of Skulls is repeated in the many tales of magic cauldrons whose chief property is to bring the dead back to life. The quest for a magical cauldron guarded in a hostile or dangerous castle is the theme of a Welsh tale of Bran the Blessed. It is found in stories of the Irish Cuchulainn and the Norse stories of Odin and Thor – all of whom succeeded in such a quest.

At least one story of the Castle of the Cauldron has some curious implications. This is the tale of the British hero Arthur who, with many companions, goes on a quest to the land of Annwn, a mysterious place whose name literally means 'not world'. Here Arthur attempts to find the Castle of the Magical Cauldron. (There is yet another, later, tale in which Arthur is actually held prisoner in a Castle of Skulls).

The early Arthur, however, is a very different man from the later king of Camelot. But it could well be that this early tale of Arthur is the source for what later became the quest for the Grail Castle, for the Castle of the Cauldron is a most amazing place. It is a magnificent glass castle, foursquare and magically revolving in an isle ringed by the heavy blue chain of the sea. It is a rich and royal castle, but is guarded by silent, ghostly sentinels and is plunged in darkness. At the castle's centre is the object of the Quest, the pearl-rimmed cauldron of poetry and inspiration attended by nine beautiful virgin priestesses.

Arthur and his men of Britain attempt to carry off the cauldron out of the mysterious otherworld of Annwn. But the perils prove so overwhelming that of all those who set out, only seven return.

THE VOYAGE OF MAEL DUIN

THE WORLD OF FAERIE is rich with magical islands. In the catalogue of island castles visited by the Irish hero Mael Duin and his band was one that was a huge silver pillar standing upright in the sea; another was called the Island Castle of the Millstone Beast. They came upon one island with magical fruit, another that appeared to be a leg standing in the sea with a great door in it. Still another was surmounted by an enchantress's castle that possessed a magical glass drawbridge.

CAER ARIANROD

OF ALL THE MAGICAL ISLAND CASTLES of Faerie, the one called Caer Arianrod that once stood in the Straits of Menai in North Wales was numbered among the most beautiful. Now only a few rocks, visible at low tide, mark the place.

This was the sea castle of the beautiful goddess and enchantress Arianrod, whose name means 'Silver Wheel'. She was both sister and mistress to the Druid of the Gods, the powerful Magician-God Gwydion. By Gwydion, Arianrod had two sons: Lleu, the god of Sun and Light, and Dylan, the god of Sea and Darkness.

For many ages, the immortal Arianrod remained in her sea-swept castle, but the hostility of Christian evangelists forced her, and Gwydion with her, to retire more and more from the lands of men. At last Gwydion could bear it no more and caused his own home and that of his sister to be lifted up above the world and into the stars.

And there, anyone versed in Welsh lore will tell you, their castles remain in the constellations. The Castle of Gwydion is that formation others call the Milky Way, while the Castle of Arianrod is that group often called the Northern Crown.

FAERIE LORE IS FILLED WITH TALES of castles and kingdoms that vanished beneath the sea. Some tell of inhabitants driven out by flood, others of their sudden and tragic drowning. Often, too, the story is of those who continue to inhabit the castles and live forever deep beneath the waves. In most cases it would appear that the engulfment by water is a punishment for the sins of the inhabitants or for the violation of a taboo.

These stories abound in the Celtic fringes of Europe. In Wales, Ireland, Cornwall and Brittany. The tales are consistent enough to suggest that there is some basis of truth in them.

Under the waters of Cardigan Bay, off the Welsh coast, lies the land of Cantref y Gwaelod (the land of the Underworld). This once was the kingdom of Gwyddneu Garanhir and its borders were protected from the sea by embankments. These were in the charge of Seithenin the Drunkard and, through his lack of care, one night the dykes were breached and the land was flooded and irretrievably lost. In this calamity sixteen fortified cities were submerged. Gwyddneu, his means drastically reduced, was forced to scrape a living from the produce of a fishing weir.

The story has it that the inebriated Seithenin had violated a girl – the guardian of a magic well – and to avenge this desecration the elemental power of the sea had overwhelmed the whole kingdom.

IN THE CORNISH LEGENDS, Lyonnesse, the land which lay to the west of Cornwall, along with all its cities and castles, was destroyed by a massive wave. One person alone, the possessor of the fastest horse in the kingdom, managed to outrun the sea and reach safety.

A few scattered fragments of rocks and the Scilly Isles are all that remain of this once proud land.

Y'S – THE CITY OF THE DEPTHS

THE KING OF CORNWALL built the magnificent Castle and
City of Y's for his daughter, the Princess Dahud. But such was
the debauchery and sin of the people in that fair place that the sea
waters came and overwhelmed it, and it became known as the
City of the Depths.

Since then, the fishermen of Cornwall have often seen the Princess Dahud
swimming beneath the sea. And when the sea is becalmed in that place, the
entire Castle and City of Y's can be seen – walls, churches, houses, towers

all unblemished and unchanged by the vast flood.

It is claimed that the bells in the Princess Chapel still sadly ring each day. And to those bells a prophecy is attached, for the first youth to hear the sound of the submerged bell will save the realm.

And in that moment, the City will be restored and emerge from its watery grave no worse than a new babe after baptism. The long vanished citizens of Y's will be revived and the Princess Dahud will wed the hero who hears the bells. And he will become the new king over Y's.

THE CASTLE OF PENTECOST

IN THE LAND OF BRITTANY there is a submerged castle
under the sands of the Côtes-du-Nord. Every year on the night
of Pentecost, the castle rises up and is only accessible for the
twelve strokes of midnight. Within the castle is the greatest of
prizes – a magician's hazel wand of absolute power – the reward for any hero
swift and brave enough to seize it. And it has been sought by many.

68

Perik Skoarn, a brave adventurer, determined to obtain the wand although
he was forewarned that there would be temptations throughout the castle to
waylay him.

Many of these temptations, such as rooms full of gold and jewels, did not
delay him in the least. And as he swept on his way, it seemed he might just
achieve his goal. Then he entered the Room of the Hundred Maidens and
knew at once that he was lost, for he immediately succumbed to their allure.

The fatal twelfth stroke of midnight struck, and the castle, and the hero
Perik – and the Hundred Maidens – all vanished beneath the sea.

THE PRINCESS AT THE WELL

KING ECCA BUILT A CASTLE on a low plain. At its centre was a beautiful garden with a magical well of perpetual crystal waters with great curative powers. However, it required a constant guardian, and this duty fell to the Princess Libane.

After some time the Princess became forgetful of her duties to the well and allowed it to flood. Soon a great lake engulfed the castle, drowning King Ecca and all his family. But the Princess survived, continuing to live in the castle under the lake. There, it is said by some, she still sits by the well, her punishment to attend forever to the duty she so fatally neglected those centuries ago. Others maintain she sits there no longer but, mercifully, was transformed into a salmon.

71

THE AGE OF ROMANCE

THE AGE OF ROMANCE began in a remote clifftop castle on the coast of Cornwall.

This was Tintagel, where Queen Igraine awaited news of the battle which her husband Gorlois was fighting against Uther Pendragon – king of the unsteady confederation of warring states which was then Britain. The war was being fought because Uther coveted Gorlois's young wife, and indeed that was why she had been hidden away in the near-impregnable fortress.

In the dusk, three figures, bearing the semblance of Gorlois and two companions, arrived at the gate and were admitted. But the real Gorlois was dead. The man Igraine slept with that night was Uther Pendragon, transformed by magic into the appearance of her husband.

The widowed Queen later gave birth to a son and christened him Arthur. The man who took the child away to be fostered and eventually brought him into his rightful inheritance was the enchanter Merlin. It was he who had aided the boy's father and he was to guide and assist the son as he rose to become the most celebrated king in the annals of Romance.

THE TITANIC FIGURE of King Arthur held sway over the whole age of Romance. To his court to offer allegiance and to fight under his dragon banner came the greatest and most illustrious knights—Sir Lancelot, Sir Gawain, Sir Bedivere, Sir Kay, Tristram of Lyonesse. From far-flung parts of the world young men, eager for fame and honour came to seek service with Arthur and hopefully be knighted by him.

In order to maintain his wide dominion Arthur held court in Wales at Caerleon, in the North at Carlisle, and in London. But the seat of his power and his most beloved home was the castle-city of Camelot.

THE ARCHITECT OF CAMELOT was the enchanter Merlin, and it was
on his advice that Arthur established that most famous alliance of knights,
the Order of the Round Table. This was the circle of power designed by
Merlin which inspired the followers of Arthur to the highest ideals of
knighthood.

   If Camelot was the embodiment of an ideal, the wide lands of the Arthurian
world were filled with powers that challenged its sovereignty. Powerful,
often evil, lords ruled over kingdoms near and distant, from many dark and
sinister castles.

The white beacon towers of Camelot shone over the barbaric lands of the age. Inspired by the ideal of chivalry, knight after knight rode out in Arthur's name to tame the world. The lonely figure of the questing knight was symbolic of the Christian conquest of a pagan world, and many a knight was confronted with stark allegorical landscapes of dark and sinister woods, forbidden valleys, dangerous and wondrous castles.

VERY MUCH IN KEEPING with these allegorical tales is the story of the Castle of Maidens, in which seven brothers represent the seven deadly sins and the maidens the souls of all those in Purgatory who were to be freed by the coming of Christ.

THE CASTLE OF MAIDENS

GO THOU NOW, adventurous knight, to the Castle of Maidens, and there do thou away the wicked customs."

This was the instruction received by Sir Galahad, the son of Lancelot, and the young knight known as the 'purest and most perfect . . .' In the Castle of Maidens, seven evil knights, having killed the rightful king and usurped his throne, held captive seven maidens of the castle until they would agree to marry the usurpers.

Any passing ladies were added to the captive group, while any accompanying knights were treacherously slain.

As Galahad neared the castle, he was met by seven maidens on white palfreys and a friar who earnestly warned him against proceeding further. It was advice he would not heed, and when he arrived before the gates of the castle he was met by seven armed knights. One by one they lowered their lances and spurred their horses to meet him in single combat. One by one Sir Galahad overthrew them and in so doing freed all the maidens in the castle.

ARTHUR'S NEPHEW, THE NOBLE SIR GAWAIN, undertook the rescue of the maidens in the amazing Castle of Wonders. This was the castle created by the evil genius of the Wizard Klingsor. Klingsor was undoubtedly one of the faeriefolk, an evil counterpart to Merlin, and equally a master-builder of magical castles.

THE CASTLE OF WONDERS

THE WIZARD KLINGSOR once cast an evil spell upon the Castle of Wonders so that all within were held in thrall to his power. They could only await a hero who might break the spell. This Sir Gawain undertook to do.

When Gawain came within sight of the castle, he saw it had five hundred windows in which five hundred sorrowing maidens awaited their rescue. Strangely, there were no guards at the gate and Gawain entered unopposed. He dismounted from his horse in the courtyard and cautiously entered one room after another in search of an adversary. At last he came to the castle's Great Hall, which, like all the other rooms, was beautifully decorated with gold, ivory, jewels and fine woods. It had a roof 'coloured like peacock plumes' but was strangely furnished with a single huge, beautifully carved bed.

Rather bemused by his lack of opposition, Gawain went to sit awhile on the bed. At once the bed moved away from under him. Picking himself up, he again tried to climb on the bed, and again it moved away. The faster he pursued it, the more rapidly the great bed skimmed over the polished ebony floor. Finally, Gawain, by making a feint, managed to leap upon it. However, he then needed to cling to the demented piece of furniture with all his strength for it careened around the Hall in such a frenzy that it crashed into walls and pillars in an effort to throw him. But the knight's grip held, and, as if admitting defeat, it came to a halt.

This, however, proved to be only the first trial, for immediately the room was filled with a hail of stones fired from powerful slings concealed around the walls. The stones battered and stunned the armoured Gawain, but did not kill him. Then, as suddenly the slings ceased their hurling, five hundred mechanical archers appeared from compartments within the walls and fired deadly arrows at the knight.

Gashed and wounded though he was by the mechanical army, by great skill and considerable luck Gawain made a desperate defence and was still able to fight when a lion, as large as a horse, leapt into the Hall. This, he felt, was something he could cope with. Knight and lion locked in battle, and with the last of his strength, Gawain managed to sever the lion's head.

The death of the lion shattered the spell over the castle, and a great sigh of release was heard throughout from the captive maidens. At once the Queen and her ladies came to Gawain in the Great Hall and greeted him as their King. He was led from the Great Hall up a winding stair to the top of the castle's tallest tower where there was a jewelled room with a marvellous pillar. In it all the lands of the kingdom could be seen at once. Every living thing that stirred in the countryside could be seen in miniature and in perfect detail on the pillar's shining surface.

While gazing fascinated into the pillar, Gawain was told that he was now master of the enchanted castle and all its lands, if he would but promise the maidens that he would never leave the realm. Though greatly tempted, Gawain proved true to his allegiance to the Round Table and chose, albeit regretfully, to return to his comrades and his king in Camelot.

THE CASTLES that we read about in the Romances can sometimes be identified with real castles, or some geographical location. 'Senaudon', for example, is Snowdon, Castle Magounes is Arundel in Sussex. Joyous Garde, Lancelot's castle, is usually identified with Bamburgh in Northumberland. Camelot itself has been variously identified with sites in Cornwall, Scotland, and Somerset, though Malory places it firmly at Winchester.

More often than not, however, the castles are situated in an unreal and fabulous landscape in which the only frontiers are between this world and the next.

The names of many of these castles – and often that is all we know of them – are wonderfully suggestive and hint at stories long forgotten: The Castle of Heavy Sorrow, The Dolorous Tower, The Castle of Four Stories, The Castle of Goothe, Castle Loñazep and Castle Pendragon.

There are several examples of castles called Orgulous, or pride. In one of these a knight called Sir La Côte Mal Taille nearly met his death. He had chased another knight into his castle and slain him, only to find the gates shut behind him and his way of retreat blocked. The rest of the knights in that castle, a hundred in number, went to avenge their lord and Sir La Côte Mal Taille had to fight them all at once. He defended himself magnificently until a maiden, who had been watching the spectacle for some time, took pity on him and let him out through a postern.

AMONG THE COUNTLESS ARTHURIAN TALES of distressed maidens held captive in castles, the story of Castle Perilous holds a certain lasting charm both because of its humble knight and its enthusiastic combination of magic and morality.

CASTLE PERILOUS

A DAMSEL CALLED LINET once came to Camelot seeking a champion who might rescue her sister, lovely Lady Lyonesse, who had for two years been beseiged in her Castle Perilous by Sir Ironside, the Red Knight of the Red Launds.

King Arthur immediately granted Linet's petition, but she was outraged when, instead of a famous knight, Arthur chose an eager kitchen knave to go on this adventure. Arthur had judged the nameless youth to be of knightly mettle, but Linet, disgusted, left the court. Unknown to any in Camelot, the young man was really Gareth of Orkney, brother to Sir Gawain and youngest nephew of Arthur.

Gareth galloped off after Linet – much to her distaste. Throughout the perilous journey she reviled him at every opportunity, even when he had overthrown three worthy foes – the Black Knight, the Green Knight and the Blue Knight – actually mocking them, indeed, for having been defeated by a lowly kitchen knave! But Gareth goodnaturedly continued to insist on protecting her.

When at last they arrived at the Castle Perilous they found it surrounded by the machinery of war. Hanging from the trees were forty unfortunate knights who had previously undertaken this quest. Undeterred by their cruel death, Gareth sounded a great ivory horn which hung from a sycamore.

Straightaway the huge Red Knight of the Red Launds charged out to answer the challenge, his helm, armour, shield, lance and even his steed all of the bloodiest red. For the most part of a day they fought in the little vale under the castle wall, where all within might see the battle. The lovely Lady Lyonesse was one of the most breathless watchers.

Eventually Gareth overpowered his opponent, splitting his helm and knocking him to the earth. Only Gareth's merciful nature stopped him from taking the Red Knight's life. The Knight, acknowledging defeat, promised to withdraw his forces and go to Arthur's court to swear obedience to the King.

Thus the siege of Castle Perilous was raised by the honourable kitchen knave. Gareth's true identity was revealed, and he and Lady Lyonesse having fallen deeply in love, they plighted their troth together.

However, once the lovers had sworn to marry, their passion was so fired with desire that the Lady made a tryst with Gareth to come to his bed that very night. And this she did. But their dalliance was interrupted by the entrance of an armed knight accompanied by a great clamour of noise and many strange glittering lights. The intruder attacked Gareth and wounded him in the thigh, but Gareth grabbed his sword and struck the knight's head off.

While Gareth's wound was being stanched, the damsel Linet, still busy protecting her sister, swiftly picked up the head and applied an ointment, then replaced the head on the fallen body. Immediately the knight returned to life, albeit somewhat shaken, and she led him away.

The next night, the same thing happened. Once more the lovers were prevented from dishonouring themselves by the ferocious knight. This time, however, Gareth cut the head of his assailant into a hundred pieces and threw them from the window. Linet patiently collected the pieces and, applying the ointment as before, reassembled the head and restored the knight to life.

The wounds suffered by Gareth in these encounters not only further delayed the lovers, but could only be healed by the lady whose enchantments had caused them. Linet did see to it that he was in full health again in time for his wedding. After which, the phantom axeman left the lovers in peace, his restless moral spirit soothed by their lawful union.

THE PERILS OF LOVE played a large part in the stories of chivalry and courtly romance. They fostered the idea that love should be earned by long periods of self-denial and by courage displayed in battle and tournaments.

In this tradition Sir Lancelot was the most popular of all Arthurian characters because, although he betrayed his King by his adultery with the Queen; he did so reluctantly, driven by passion, and his devotion to Guinevere was complete and lifelong.

Possibly the most extreme expression of this love is the tale of the Castle of Gorre. Gorre was one of those kingdoms 'whence no foreigner returns', and clearly has implications of the otherworld realm so often come across in pagan myth and frequently identified with an underworld or Christian Purgatory.

THE CASTLE OF GORRE

IN THE KINGDOM OF GORRE, whence no man might return, was a powerful knight called Meliagante, son to the King of that land, who so craved the Lady Guinevere that he contrived to abduct her and took her away to his castle.

Sir Lancelot furiously pursued the evil Meliagante, but found that to enter the land of Gorre he must cross a deep, swift river. He chose the most difficult crossing, which was the Sword Bridge, a gigantic weapon lying from bank to bank, razor-edge uppermost. Moreover, two leopards, chained to a rock, guarded the far shore.

The better to prove his ardour, Lancelot deliberately removed the mail and armour from his hands and feet before crawling across the cruel bridge. Terribly wounded when he reached the other side, he nevertheless attempted to rise to fight the leopards guarding the far bank, when he discovered the creatures were merely an illusion.

The King of Gorre was delighted by the bravery shown by Lancelot, but Meliagante, his treacherous and evil son, felt no pleasure in seeing his enemy still alive. The King tried to make peace between Lancelot and his son, but Meliagante refused to give up the Queen, so Lancelot, despite his dreadful wounds, challenged the Prince of Gorre to fight on the following day.

The next day, all the people who were captive in that land crowded around the castle square as Meliagante and their deliverer prepared to do battle.

So fiercely and hotly did the battle between the two knights rage through the day that the King at last begged Guinevere to stop them. Lancelot heard her call from her window in the tower and at once ceased to defend himself, even though his enemy continued to rain blows on him. But finally a truce was made. Guinevere and all who were imprisoned in that land were released on condition that Lancelot and Meliagante should fight for Guinevere a year later at Camelot.

Even the foul Meliagante could not again attack the sorely wounded Lancelot, but he perceived an advantage in this lapse of time. Treacherously, during that year, he entrapped Lancelot and imprisoned him in a windowless tower.

But Meliagante reckoned without the ferocity occasioned by Lancelot's overpowering love, through which the knight won to freedom and at the last possible moment appeared on the field of honour to fight for his Lady.

Although exhausted, the sight of Meliagante drove Lancelot into a battle-frenzy in which he showered vicious blows on the evil knight. So Sir Lancelot proved once again that in battle no knight in this world or from any other could stand before him. Meliagante, the Prince of Gorre, was battered into the ground and slain.

THE ENCHANTRESS CASTLES

FOR THE CHIVALROUS KNIGHT-ERRANT the rescuing of maidens sometimes proved even more perilous than was immediately apparent. Danger often came from a totally unexpected source.

In Arthurian romance the most dangerous of foes were not the giants, wizards, or even dragons. They were the apparently frail damsels who practiced the black arts – the enchantresses. Consequently, it often happened that an unwary knight would attempt to rescue some sad maiden-in-distress, only to find rather too late that he himself was her chosen victim.

THE ENCHANTRESSES were an insatiable lot and all seemed to possess wonderful castles. Their major purpose appeared to be to waylay the chivalrous knight, to divert him from his duties and draw him away from the righteous concerns of the world. The sorcerous ladies were always possessed of unearthly beauty – or at least, so they appeared. Their chief delight seemed to be to seduce a hero and then imprison him or even slay him, depending on the whim of the moment.

One of the most virtuous of Arthur's knights, Sir Bors, once came upon the castle of such an Enchantress. The beautiful lady attempted first to seduce Sir Bors, but finding that this had little effect, she resorted to more drastic tactics to delay him. With twelve other beautiful damsels she climbed the highest tower in the castle. There they all stood in the windows and on the ramparts and threatened to cast themselves down if Sir Bors would not agree to the Queen's demands.

However, Sir Bors proved to be a knight of steadfast, not to say totally inflexible, principle, and decided his holy quest must take precedence over concern for the Queen and her ladies. So when he turned to ride off, the Queen and all twelve maidens furiously hurled themselves shrieking to the ground. A moment before they struck the rocks, the maidens, the Queen, and the castle itself, all disappeared in a flash and a puff of smoke.

Knights like Sir Bors – and the equally uncompromising Sir Galahad – proved the exception, however, when it came to enchantresses. Very few others proved immune to their wiles.

The tale of the Tower of Annowre tells how King Arthur himself was once entrapped when he encountered a frail maid in a dark and mysterious forest.

This was the enchantress Annowre who, with subtle guile, persuaded Arthur to place a gift ring on his finger. The ring was magical and had the property of making Arthur become enthralled with the beautiful Annowre, who then enticed Arthur through the forest to her ruined tower where she quickly seduced him.

After the seduction, Arthur discovered the power of the ring and became disenchanted. But the cunning Annowre had two strong henchmen overpower the unarmed king. Treacherously she then attempted to murder the helpless Arthur. And indeed she would have succeeded in doing so had it not been for the sudden and timely arrival of Sir Tristram. The valiant Tristram saved his king and slew the would-be assassins.

THE CASTLE OF MORGAN LE FAY

THE MOST FAMOUS ENCHANTRESS of the age was Morgan Le Fay, the faerie half-sister to King Arthur. Among the most fascinating and powerful figures in romance, she is the beautiful and dangerous counterpart to Merlin. As Merlin is Arthur's guardian and adviser, so Morgan is his tormentor, and, through the person of their son, his eventual nemesis.

Morgan's concerns were with the faerie otherworld, sometimes called Avalon. She tried to draw Arthur into that alluring, changeless world of immortal spirits, but while he remained bound to Camelot she could only wreak havoc and mischief.

Morgan possessed numerous castles of enchantment, all equally dangerous for the unwary knight. By her beauty and her many magical skills Morgan Le Fay seduced and entrapped innumerable powerful knights. Those she favoured became her lovers, while others simply languished in her dungeons.

Among Morgan's castles were Belle Garde, Castle Chariot and the strange Castle of the Valley of No Return. This structure was the classic enchantress's castle. A place of apparent beauty, peace, luxury and sensual ease – and a false paradise that was in reality a prison. The spell of enchantment that Morgan cast about this castle and valley was that no knight who was unfaithful in word, thought or deed could ever leave.

It was the great Lancelot, with his steadfast devotion to Guinevere, who alone broke the spell. However, in doing so he earned a terrible enemy in Morgan, much to his later cost. In time even Lancelot fell victim to Morgan. For one day she discovered him sleeping beneath an apple tree and cast a spell on him. When he awoke he found himself within her castle. Morgan and three other Queens asked Lancelot to choose between them, but Lancelot rejected them all, preferring imprisonment to dishonour.

CASTLE CHARIOT

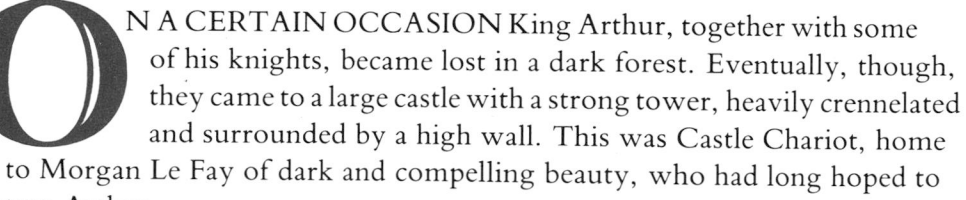

ON A CERTAIN OCCASION King Arthur, together with some of his knights, became lost in a dark forest. Eventually, though, they came to a large castle with a strong tower, heavily crennelated and surrounded by a high wall. This was Castle Chariot, home to Morgan Le Fay of dark and compelling beauty, who had long hoped to trap Arthur.

So it was with unfeigned pleasure that Morgan welcomed her half-brother and invited him and his retinue within. The walls of the courtyard were hung with tapestries and lit by countless candles: and a great company of richly dressed folk, along with the beautiful Morgan, lavishly celebrated Arthur's presence.

However, this was the same castle in which Sir Lancelot had previously been immured. For nearly two years Morgan had held him in a windowless

room, and during that time he had tried to distract himself by painting the walls of the chamber with murals that chronicled his adventures. In his loneliness and believing himself forever imprisoned he also painted in passionate detail glorious images of his beloved Guinevere, graphically celebrating his undying, adulterous love for the Queen.

Morgan saw the deadly use she could make of these murals now that she had Arthur within her walls. Soon she led the unsuspecting King into Lancelot's old quarters and left him there, knowing he would examine the paintings and come to a bitter conclusion about his wife's faithlessness and the duplicity of one of his most trusted and beloved companions.

Thus Morgan contrived to sow the seeds of discord in the fertile land of Camelot. The scandal of Lancelot and Arthur's Queen would bring forth terrible fruit, and the disintegration of the brotherhood of the Round Table would begin.

103

THE LADY OF THE LAKE

LTHOUGH Lancelot was held captive and finally betrayed by
the grand enchantress Morgan Le Fay, in childhood he had known
another beautiful sorceress who was his guardian and protector.
This was the Fay Vivien, known as the Lady of the Lake, who lived in her
castle beneath the surface of an illusory lake. This same enchantress gave to
King Arthur the magical sword Excalibur, the greatest weapon of the age.
Its blade would win victory for whoever wielded it, and its scabbard
protected from any wound the warrior who wore it.

As a baby Lancelot was brought to Vivien's faerie castle and there raised
to manhood, when the enchantress supplied him with armour and weapons
of war and reluctantly allowed him to seek service with King Arthur. The
Lady of the Lake was, quite literally, Lancelot's fairy-godmother. But once
she had raised and set him on his way she seemed to take no further interest
in his welfare.

And indeed, like Morgan Le Fay, the Lady of the Lake had many faces.
The ways of the faerie folk were ever their own, their concerns and loyalties
not with mortals. They were of a mischievous nature, the more powerful
among them driven by passionate whim. So although the Lady of the Lake
gifted Arthur's realm with its greatest weapon and its finest warrior, thereby
helping immeasurably to build the strength and power of Camelot, she was
also the enchantress who deprived the kingdom of its most powerful
guardian, the wise Merlin.

MERLIN AND THE TOWER OF AIR

EVEN THE GREAT WIZARD MERLIN, architect and powerful guardian of Camelot, was not immune to the allure of an enchantress, for he was bewitched by the beauty of Vivien, the Lady of the Lake. Indeed he was quite helpless to prevent his enthralment with Vivien and more and more gave himself over to a passionate, hopeless love for the faerie.

Through the many years of his infatuation with the lovely creature, Vivien wheedled out of him all the wizard might teach her of magic. As she grew more and more powerful, he became more and more obsessed with his passion for her.

When at last she believed she could learn no more from the master magician, she grew tired of him and of his constant attentions and plotted to be rid of him.

To achieve this end, she led Merlin deep within the enchanted forest of Brocielande and had him sit down for a time to rest beneath a thorn tree. There she used Merlin's own magic on him. Putting him in a sleeping trance, she trailed her wimple nine times around the thorn tree under which he lay. She created a 'Tower of Air' from which Merlin could never emerge.

Although Vivien could come and go as she pleased in this ensorcelled Tower of Air, to all others it was invisible. However, it is said that to this day a voice may be heard by those who wander in the ancient wood of Brocielande – the faint and distant voice of Merlin among the branches of the trees calling out and bewailing his fate.

THE MANY MYSTERIOUS, often illusory Otherworld Castles of Faerie, like those of the enchantresses, permeated Arthurian legends. However, one illusory castle grew in the centuries of telling into the most famous tale in Christian lore: the Castle of the Holy Grail.

In its earliest manifestations, the Castle of the Grail is known as the Castle of the Maimed King. It is an eerie and magnificent castle which, most of the time, is invisible and can never be found by any who attempt to seek it. Consequently it is discovered unintentionally by the young and extremely naive Sir Percivale (Parsi-fal = 'pure fool'). Unaware of the Castle's magical properties, the young Percivale attempts to behave in what he believes to be a knightly manner while a guest in this strange castle.

THE CASTLE OF THE MAIMED KING

WHEN VERY YOUNG and of the utmost innocence, Sir Percivale came upon the Castle of the Maimed King. Treated as an honoured guest, he was brought to a great feasting hall where a brotherhood of knights sat around their King who was suffering from a terrible wound that would not heal.

Naturally concerned as to the cause of the King's pain, Percivale nevertheless restrained himself from asking because he had been instructed that it was improper to ask too many questions of one's host. Soon the glowing, gold and jewelled 'Grail' was brought into the hall by a beautiful maiden. This 'Grail' was by varying accounts a stone, a dish, and finally a glowing cup. Whatever its nature, the wonderful object was a radiant cornucopia that fed all within the hall to a sumptuous feast.

Once again amazed, Percivale nevertheless held his tongue and did not comment on the Grail's astonishing performance.

After spending a night in the great castle, Percivale awoke in the morning to find the place deserted. In the courtyard he mounted his horse and rode away. Immediately the drawbridge was raised behind him and the castle vanished entirely from sight.

Later, Percivale learned that because he showed no Christian concern for the pain of the Maimed King, and no curiosity about the ultimate Christian mystery – the Grail – he had failed the test of the Great Quest. It was revealed that the mysterious castle was in fact his birthright, that had he shown sympathy for the King's suffering as any Christian might for Christ's suffering; and had he shown awe and wonder whilst in the presence of the mystery of the Grail as any Christian might in the glowing presence of the mystery of the Holy Ghost, the Quest would have been achieved.

But because of his ignorance of his Christian duties, he had caused the King unnecessary pain. Hence, the whole realm must become a terrible Waste Land of suffering and despair where nothing would grow and no bird sing.

IN EARLY VERSIONS OF THE MAIMED KING, the hunt for the Grail is more of an individual quest of the youthful Percivale and his coming into his inheritance. These tales are also permeated with the symbols and trappings of pagan religion and fertility rites, only thinly veiled by Christian symbolism.

In later stories, the Castle of the Holy Grail is known as Carbonek and its grandeur has so increased that it is the Earthly Paradise attended by angels and marvellous spirits. The Grail itself is more specifically a Christian relic: it is now a glowing Chalice – both the Chalice of the Last Supper and the Chalice in which Joseph of *Arimathaea* caught up the blood of the crucified Christ. The Holy Grail itself in its pulsing light contains the ultimate mystery. It will reveal to the master of the Quest 'what no mortal heart can devise, nor terrestrial tongue describe'.

The Quest to find Carbonek, the Grail Castle, became the supreme duty of all the knights of Arthur's Round Table. Many knights tried and failed to achieve the ultimate goal.

CARBONEK – CASTLE OF THE HOLY GRAIL

SIR LANCELOT realised that he could not achieve the Quest of the mysteriously elusive Grail Castle by force of arms. Increasingly, it became clear to him that the Quest was a spiritual one. He assumed the penance of becoming a hermit, wandering in the wilderness, fasting and praying.

In time there appeared to him a ghostly ship sailing by moonlight without captain or crew. He boarded the vessel and in the dim light found he had been taken to a rocky cliff on which stood the long sought Carbonek, Castle of the Holy Grail.

Out of the darkness a voice commanded him to enter. But at the entrance were two lions. Lancelot first tried to draw his sword but it was struck from his hand and the voice bade him enter. He went forward and entered unmolested. Within he heard a voice of unearthly beauty singing. Then a door to a chapel was opened to reveal a brilliant light. He was commanded not to enter, being tainted with the sin of his adultery with Guinevere, but because of his courageous spirit he was permitted to see the holy object from a distance.

Within Lancelot could see the brilliantly glowing Grail on a table of silver, covered with a cloth of red samite, with winged angels hovering about a mysterious priest celebrating high mass.

This was the magnificent vision granted the hero. So great was his yearning to see it more clearly that he stepped forward. He was instantly struck down with a blast of fire and lay for twenty-four days in a death-like coma before he could rise again and depart forever from Carbonek. For now he knew that because of his earthly and unholy love for the Queen he would never achieve the Quest.

IN THE END, IT WAS NONE OF THE GREAT campaigners of Arthur's Court who won the Grail Quest, but a late-arriving knight of the Round Table. This was the 'purest' knight of the brotherhood, the Red Cross Knight, Sir Galahad. He was the son of Sir Lancelot and of Elaine, daughter of the Grail King.

GALAHAD AND THE GRAIL

GALAHAD, LIKE HIS FATHER, was a matchless knight, but he was also of stainless character, so filled with Christian virtue that sin could find no place in him to thrive.

Entering Carbonek with two companions, the good Sir Bors and Sir Percivale, his courage and faultless goodness allowed him to kneel before the Holy Grail and pray for the pain of the Maimed King to cease. At once the King's wounds were healed, and all there saluted Galahad as the master of the Quest and new King.

However, the Quest was not of this world, but rather of the spirit. When at last the mantle of samite was drawn back from the Chalice and Galahad was permitted to gaze fully into the indescribable mystery, the knight found he had no desire to remain in this world. Increasingly filled with the wonder of the miracle, he became more and more a spiritual being, until at last his body was borne aloft by angels high to the gates of heaven. And with him the Grail itself ascended as well.

THE SIEGE OF JOYOUS GARDE

ITH THE QUEST OF THE HOLY GRAIL achieved, and the Grail itself departed, the spiritual centre of the Round Table seemed to disintegrate. In Camelot, the brotherhood was greatly depleted by the loss of Percivale, Galahad, and many another brave pilgrim who had embarked on the journey. Then, too, the wise counsel of Merlin was sorely missed by the King, for there was much turmoil and discord within his realm.

Finally, the revelation of his Queen's love for Lancelot sparked the flame of an inferno that would consume Arthur's kingdom and, in the end, all the flower of chivalry.

By rule of law, Guinevere had been condemned to be burned as a witch. This Lancelot would not allow, even knowing that he must defy his king. On the day of execution, Lancelot, with his kinsmen Sir Bors, Sir Lionel and Sir Hector, rescued Guinevere from the stake. But in the ensuing battle, Lancelot unwittingly slew the young Sir Gareth, brother to his great friend Gawain.

The death of Gareth, combined with the seizing of Guinevere, added the aspect of a blood-feud to the dispute that now escalated into a civil war.

Lancelot and his kinsmen and allies retreated to his Castle of Joyous Garde against which Gawain and Arthur then carried out a long and bloody siege. In the futility and despair of the conflict Lancelot renamed his castle Dolorous Garde.

Even the intervention of the Pope and the banishment of Lancelot to France could not stop the strife, for Arthur and Gawain pursued him until they forced Lancelot to stand and fight. Gawain died as a result of wounds from this duel, but worse yet, while the conflict continued in France, Mordred, the evil offspring of Arthur and his half-sister Morgan Le Fay, seized both the crown and the Queen. Arthur, with his sadly depleted forces, returned from France and on Salisbury Plain fought the bitter battle that eclipsed the remaining knighthood of England.

On Salisbury Plain all the knights on either side were slain, except for Sir Bedivere. He attended the fatally wounded Arthur after the King had given the death blow to his traitorous son Mordred. On Arthur's order Bedivere hurled Excalibur into the lake near the battleground. Miraculously a hand rose to take it, and soon after, a barge appeared bearing Morgan Le Fay and the Lady of the Lake, who took up the wounded king and sailed into the mists of Avalon.

Many believe he rules still with Morgan in the faerie kingdom of Avalon. Other tales tell of other places where the body of Arthur lies – beneath Glastonbury Tor, or at Glastonbury Cathedral, reunited with Guinevere, where an inscription is carved, 'Here lies Arthur, king once and king to be'.

A Welsh folk tradition claims he and all his knights did not die but sleep in a cave beneath Snowdon where they await a call from their country in its hour of need, while at Cadbury Castle in Somerset, Arthur and his men are said to lie sleeping fully armed under the hill. Sometimes at night the beat of horses' hooves can be heard as they ride down to a spring. And in the north of England a legend says that Arthur and Guinevere sleep deep beneath Sewingshields Castle in Northumberland, awaiting the call.

CHARLEMAGNE

JUST AS KING ARTHUR became the Hero of Britain and his castle of Camelot the centre of a great cycle of legends, so in France the historic figure of the Holy Roman Emperor Charlemagne and his court of Aix-la-Chapelle became the centre of a great romance cycle of its own. Like Arthur's Knights of the Round Table at Camelot, Charlemagne also gathered about him an alliance of questing Palladins.

Aix-la-Chapelle was considered the most beautiful court in Europe, and in keeping with the avowed faith of the Holy Roman Emperor, contained the richest chapel to the Virgin in all France. However, the tale of the building of Aix-la-Chapelle itself is not at all Christian. It is a story of pagan magic and high romance.

AIX-LA-CHAPELLE

ALL-CONQUERING IN WAR, Charlemagne was yet dogged by tragedy; for the Emperor's first three queens died while very young. Grieving for the death of his last queen, Charlemagne believed he would never marry again. However, his counsellors, wishing both for his happiness and for a secure succession, sent for the Eastern Princess Frastrada, said to be the most beautiful woman in all the Orient.

At the first sight of Frastrada, the Emperor immediately fell in love, and declared that she would be his new Queen. It was not, however, merely Frastrada's beauty which compelled Charlemagne's love. Frastrada wore a magical gold ring, and by its power Charlemagne was bound to love and desire any who possessed it.

Through the compulsion of this ring, Queen Frastrada won the most devoted affection of Charlemagne. He could never bear to be parted from her, and for many years they were happy and the Empire prospered. In time, however, an epidemic swept France and Frastrada became ill. Try as he could, the mighty Charlemagne could do nothing to save his adored Queen. Desperate, he watched as life faded from her.

Yet even in death, the spell of the ring did not abate. Frastrada was to have been buried in a tomb in the cathedral of Mayence, but Charlemagne refused to be parted from his love and her body was laid out in a chamber where he could be with her day and night. The power of the ring compelled him to see her as beautiful as she had been in life, and so he watched over her, wasting away and neglecting the affairs of state.

Finally, Bishop Turpin, the Emperor's trusted first minister, came to the chamber whilst Charlemagne lay in a fitful sleep and discovered the enchanted ring. Wishing to release his beloved Emperor from its spell, Turpin took the ring from the dead Queen and slipped it on his own hand.

When Charlemagne awoke, he found the better part of his consuming grief had passed from him and ordered the burial of his Queen. He then began to attend to the matters of his Empire, but found himself constantly seeking the counsel of Bishop Turpin. The first minister's judgement in all matters now seemed essential to Charlemagne; it was obvious to him that Turpin was the wisest and best of men. Indeed, he could not bear to be parted from the Bishop at any time.

Rather daunted by the realization that the power of the ring could arouse in Charlemagne an obsession for a man fully as strong as that for a woman, Turpin nonetheless took advantage of the situation in order to restore Charlemagne's health and strengthen the Empire. After some time, however, even the faithful Turpin found Charlemagne's devotion rather too burdensome, but fearful that the ring might fall into another's hands he thought carefully on what he might do to dispose of it.

Late one night, Turpin decided on a course of action. Mounting his horse he rode deep into a great forest until at last in the heart of the wood he came upon a beautiful lake whose surface perfectly reflected the moon and the stars. Without hesitation he took the ring from his hand and threw it into the centre of the lake.

Still, though no person now commanded the ring, its power over the Emperor would not be denied. Charlemagne was destined to be under its spell for all of his life. In ways he could not know, it haunted him. His nights now were restless, his days distracted, and his shifting moods would not allow him to concentrate on government.

One day, he called for his huntsmen, hoping that the exercise of the chase might dispel his restlessness. But once in the forest, the Emperor found he was drawn further and further away from his huntsmen and their spot. At last he came to a glade where he discovered that same beautiful mirroring pool where Turpin had thrown the ring.

Joy filled Charlemagne at the sight of the crystal lake. He was enraptured by the beauty of the lake and its surroundings and, inexplicably, he felt as though he were coming home. In a daze he descended from his horse and settled on the margin of the water, gazing into its clear depths. Looking into the deep pool Charlemagne saw a faerie vision of tall elegant towers arising from the waters. His heart burst with love for this place, and he proclaimed that he would build the greatest castle of all his domains and the finest chapel to the Virgin on this spot.

This was to be Aix-la-Chapelle, the capital of Charlemagne's realm, and, unbeknownst to him, the last resting place of the power that had bound him to his lovely Queen.

CHARLEMAGNE AND PAMPLONA

CHARLEMAGNE was the first great monarch to organize all his forces in an effort to drive the Moors from Spain. But his Holy War cost him dear, for his favourite nephew and the greatest Palladin, Roland, was killed in the Valley of Thorns in the Pyrenèes.

Charlemagne avenged the death of Roland with a terrible slaughter of the Saracen forces. And when the Christian army marched on the Moorish castles, they fell one by one to his righteous sword. In all, thirty castles were conquered by Charlemagne in Spain before he came to the greatest of the Moorish strongholds, the Castle of Pamplona.

Here Charlemagne's army fought and besieged the Saracens for months without any sign of their weakening. The infidels remained as defiant as ever within the protective walls of the stronghold, and the Christians despaired of conquering their enemies.

But inspired by his great faith, Charlemagne at last climbed a hill before the walls and kneeled down to pray for a miracle by which the infidels might be delivered to him. As he prayed he heard a thunderous sound, and looking up, he saw the walls of Pamplona – like the ancient walls of Jericho – come crashing down. The path to Pamplona was opened before him and the Holy Roman Emperor of Christendom entered in bloody triumph.

ALTHOUGH THE POPE HIMSELF had appointed Charlemagne the Holy
Roman Emperor, the great monarch was not always at peace with the
Christian kings and princes of Europe. Indeed, even within his alliance of
Palladins there were many bloody conflicts.

Such quarrels led to tragic events: the death of brave Renaud of
Montaubon, the exile of Huon of Bordeaux, and Charlemagne's own
blood-feud with the heroic Dane, Ogier.

CHARLEMAGNE AND OGIER, THE DANE

FOR MANY YEARS Ogier the Dane served Charlemagne valiantly and well and was numbered amongst the greatest Palladins of Europe. However, a quarrel in the Emperor's court resulted in the death of Ogier's son at the hand of Charlemagne's son, Charlot. This so embittered Ogier that when Charlemagne went to war with the King of Lombardy, Ogier went over to the enemy and fought in defence of Lombard Castle.

The Lombard garrison, however, proved no match for Charlemagne's forces. Only the demonic strength and courage of Ogier managed to organize any semblance of resistance. Even so, Ogier found the defenders falling one by one about him in the Castle keep where they made their last stand. But as his men fell, Ogier dressed pieces of wood in their helmets and armour so that the defenders on the battlements appeared to remain numerous despite the terrible onslaught.

From the Castle keep, for an entire day and a night, the lone hero Ogier ferociously fought off the whole army of the Emperor with a garrison of dead men.

At last the blood-feud rage of the heroes burned so hot that even heaven became alarmed and sent down an angel to mediate between them. The angel commanded that an oath of peace be sworn between Ogier and Charlemagne. It was a command that neither Christian could disobey and each was secretly glad to make. Indeed, Charlemagne and Ogier were sincerely reconciled, and Ogier eventually became the hero Danske, over his domain from the to Charlemagne all the rest of his and king of Denmark, presiding, as Holger Castle of Elsinore. And he remained loyal days.

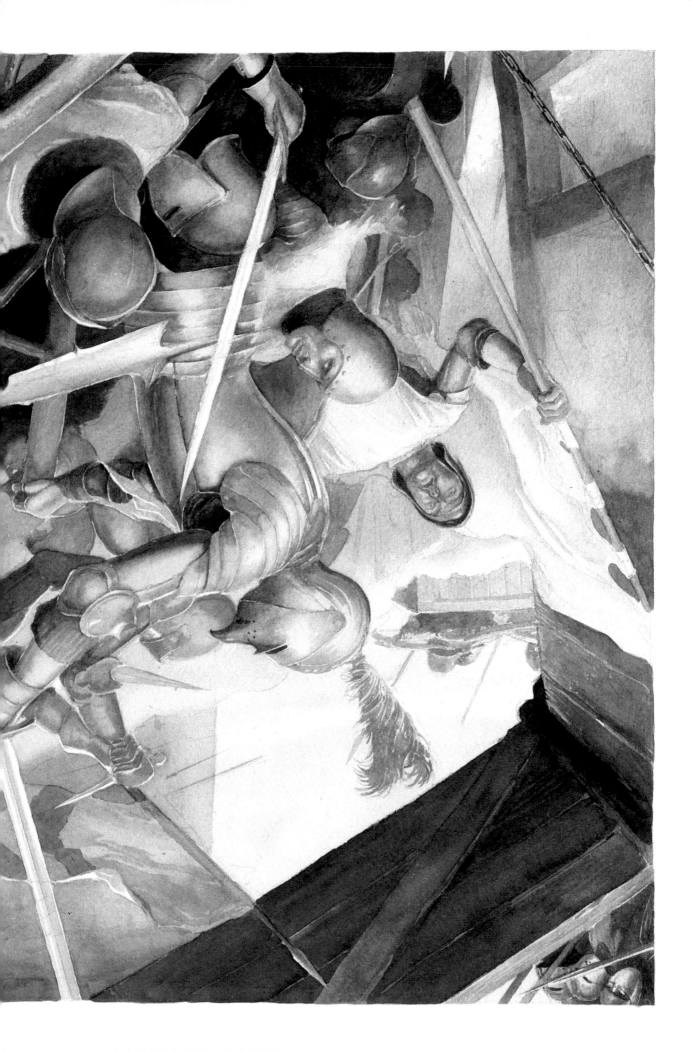

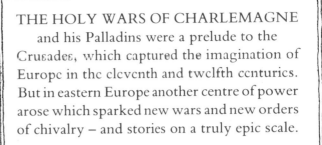

THE HOLY WARS OF CHARLEMAGNE
and his Palladins were a prelude to the
Crusades, which captured the imagination of
Europe in the eleventh and twelfth centuries.
But in eastern Europe another centre of power
arose which sparked new wars and new orders
of chivalry – and stories on a truly epic scale.

THE RHINE CASTLES

THE RHINE VALLEY is the heartland of German castle lore. Even today a journey down the Rhine transports the traveller to the age of mediaeval romance, as mountain top after mountain top reveals one castle after another.

Once the dominant power of Rhineland was centred in the Burgundian Castle at Worms. The historic rise to power of the Burgundian princes and their total annihilation at the hands of Attila's Huns is at the core of the national epic of the German people, the *Nibelungenlied* – the epic which, combined with the Volsung Saga, formed the basis for Wagner's great opera, *The Ring Cycle*.

SIEGFRIED AND THE RHINE CASTLES

IN THE CASTLE of the Burgundians of Worms-on-the-Rhine, there lived the fairest maiden in Rhineland, the Princess Kriemhild. From all Germany knights came to the high-walled city of her brother King Gunther, in hope of winning her hand. Among them was the greatest warrior of the age, Siegfried the Dragon-Slayer, who was king of the Netherlands Castle of Xanten on the far reaches of the Rhine.

For love of Kriemhild, Siegfried became an ally of King Gunther. And when the kingdom was attacked by two huge invading armies of Saxons and Danes, Siegfried joined them in battle. Largely through the efforts of the Dragon-Slayer, the Burgundians crushed their enemies and won military supremacy of all Rhineland. Moreover, with Siegfried's vast wealth – the great Nibelungen treasure of rhinegold – the Burgundians now shared the greatest riches in Europe. And finally, when Siegfried wedded Kriemhild, and Gunther, for his part, wedded Brunhild the Amazon Queen of Iceland, the Burgundian dynasty and the Rhineland alliance of Worms and Xanten seemed secure and indomitable.

However, a jealous quarrel arose between the two Queens, and the greedy desire of the Burgundians to possess totally the Nibelung treasure led to tragedy.

King Gunther and his iron-willed uncle Hagen treacherously murdered the valiant Siegfried and, seizing the Nibelung treasure, filled the whole of Worms' greatest and most secure tower with its gold and gems. Not wishing his sister Kriemhild, Siegfried's widow, to spread dissent within the realm, King Gunther sent her to the court of Etzel, the Emperor of the Huns. There, in the great Castle Gram on the banks of the Danube, the widowed Kriemhild was married to the Hun Emperor. And though Etzel proved a kindly and loving husband, Kriemhild could not be reconciled with her brother. She was consumed by an obsession for revenge, and the once fair and meek maiden was tranformed into an avenging fury.

With a pretence of forgiveness, Kriemhild invited the whole of the Burgundian knighthood to a celebration and feast within the Castle Gram. Once there Kriemhild had all of the squires put to death, thus provoking a battle with the knights within the banquet hall.

The frenzy of this battle was without parallel. The feasting hall became a slaughterhouse, the floor flooded with blood and piled with human heads and limbs. The doors and stairs were blocked with bodies, and the Huns had to climb over the dead to enter the hall. They fought on into the night, when

Kriemhild ordered the hall to be set to the torch. Many died in the flames, but a remnant of the Burgundians took refuge under the stone arches of the hall, drank the blood of the slain to slake their thirst, and fought on.

In the end, however, the Huns triumphed – but at a terrible cost. All the Burgundian knighthood was slaughtered, and the Burgundian royal line wiped out. Gunther and Hagen, and even Kriemhild, met a violent and treacherous end in this web of murder and intrigue.

This was the holocaust that ended forever the power of the Burgundians on the Rhine. What remained of this people abandoned their Castle at Worms and fled westward and settled in that region of France which today bears their name. And as for the great Nibelung treasure that was the cause of so much strife, Gunther and Hagen hid it in some secret place deep in the Rhine River itself.

If castles there be beneath the waters of the Rhine, then there will you find the gold and gems of the Nibelung horde, for no man ever found that treasure, though legends tell that the water faeries – the Rhine maidens and Nixies – make sport of swimming and playing amid the glittering prize that brought grief to so many mortal souls.

AFTER THE HIGH TRAGEDY of German epic, the tales that built up around that supreme figure of German romance, Dietrich of Verona, took on a glamour that is less tragic and more magical.
Dietrich was based on the historic figure of the Emperor Theodoric the Goth, and is the German counterpart of Arthur of Britain and Charlemagne of France. A peerless warrior, Dietrich ruled from his castle in Verona, but sought out adventures in Otherworld castle-kingdoms of Mountain Giants, Dwarfs and Faeries. The castles in Dietrich's romances drift toward high fantasy. Among the many adventures of Dietrich is the tale of the Ice Castle of Jeraspunt.

DIETRICH AND THE CASTLE OF THE ICE QUEEN

IN HIS WANDERINGS, Dietrich of Verona once entered the realm of a race of Mountain Giants ruled over by Orkis, the cannibal Giant, and his evil son, Janibas the Wizard. Dietrich learned that the Giants were making war on the highest mountain kingdom of the Ice-Faeries in the snow-peaked Alps. This was the domain of the magical snowmaidens who were ruled by Virginal, the Ice Queen, from her glittering Castle of Jeraspunt, the highest peak in the Alps.

Dietrich carried out a long campaign of war on the Mountain Giants, slaying one after the other and taking mountain castle after mountain castle. In one such encounter, he met and killed the terrible Orkis himself. However, when he arrived within sight of the Ice Castle, he found the way barred by the son of the Giant King – a foe far more formidable than the dead Orkis. For Janibas the Wizard had laid siege to the shining Castle with an awesome army of Giants, evil men, and monsters. To his foes, Janibas appeared as a phantom black rider who commanded tempests and was backed by demons and black hell-hounds. But the Wizard's most terrifying power was the ability to command those who were slain in battle to rise up from the dead and fight again.

131

Beyond his ambition to seize the realm of the Ice Queen and the Ice Castle, Janibas's main driving desire was to enhance his sorcerer's powers by taking possession of the magical jewel in the crown of the Ice Queen. For by the powers of this jewel she could command the elements in the lands of ice and snow, and by it she ruled the mountains.

Dietrich could see the seige army lying like a black sea around the many-towered Ice Castle. It was obvious that, however well defended, the Castle must eventually fall to the never-dwindling numbers of the sorcerer's army. Despite what would seem an impossible task, Dietrich was spurred to a battle-frenzy by the sight of the beautiful Ice Queen on the battlements of the tallest tower. Her radiance matched even that of the star-like jewel dancing in her crown with icy light.

In a valiant attempt to raise the seige
Dietrich slaughtered all before him,
but this proved futile as the dead simply
rose up to fight again. Dietrich then
decided on another strategy. Seeing that
Janibas commanded his forces by
means of a sorcerer's iron tablet held
aloft, Dietrich pursued the Black
Horseman himself. Striking Janibas down
from his phantom steed, Dietrich
lifted his sword and smashed the iron tablet.
As the tablet broke, the glaciers
of the mountains split and shattered,
thundering down in massive avalanches
that buried forever the whole evil host
of Giants and phantoms and un-dead.

Dietrich triumphantly made his way
to the Castle as the gates were flung
open to greet him. He was welcomed by
the incomparable Ice Queen herself,
surrounded by her dazzling court of
snowmaidens, all aglow with fairy light
and the glitter of diamond veils.
Here in the Ice Castle of Jeraspunt, in the
realm of the Ice Faeries,
Dietrich and the Ice Queen were wed.

DIETRICH AND THE DWARF-KING'S CASTLE

THE DWARF-KING LAURIN dwelt in the splendid towers of his castle perched on high crags above a secret Alpine valley in the Tyrolean Mountains. The Castle had a huge iron gate which opened onto a golden door. Both gate and door were forged by the matchless skills of the dwarfsmiths and were believed to be impassable by any enemy. The Castle's great halls and many subterranean chambers were not illuminated with torches, but with magic glowing gemstones.

Here Laurin, the King of Dwarfs, was an all-powerful monarch, and here he had taken the beautiful Princess Simult after he had abducted her.

When Dietrich learned of the plight of the Princess he immediately went with three heroic companions into the Tyrolean Mountains to attempt to free her. Even Dietrich recognized that it might be foolish to try to storm the Dwarf-King's Castle. However, Dietrich had learned of a means by which he might bring the Dwarf-King out.

It seems that above all things in the world Laurin valued his fabulous ever-flowering Rose Garden that lay in the valley just beyond his Castle walls. The magical garden had four golden gates, but was protected by a 'wall' that consisted of only a single silken thread. However, there were few who dared enter the garden, for it was well known that trespassers would pay a terrible penalty. The Dwarf-King would sever the right hand and the right foot of any transgressor.

So it was here, in the magical Rose Garden, that Dietrich and his companions chose to challenge the Dwarf-King. They rode into the garden, snapping the silken thread and trampling the roses underfoot. Instantly there was a sound like thunder and the Dwarf-King appeared on a powerful horse, armed with a great sword and dressed in glittering armour.

The effect on the heroes was not one of awe or fear, however, but of such disbelief that they very nearly collapsed in laughter. For despite the anger of the Dwarf-King and his brilliant accoutrements of war, the battle-hardened veterans could not take seriously the threats of any being who, in full armour, did not even measure three feet in height.

Their mirth was a near fatal error, for Laurin's powers proved truly devastating. Furious at their helpless laughter, the Dwarf-King instantly wrapped himself in his cloak of invisibility and leapt unseen among the warriors. Armed with an invincible sword and a belt that gave him the strength of twelve men, he totally overcame two of Dietrich's companions before Dietrich managed to close with him. Even the great hero found the Dwarf-King more than a match, and it was only by chance that he managed to grip the sword-arm of the invisible Laurin and force him to drop his weapon. Even so, Dietrich was nearly overthrown by the enormous strength of the invisible demon as they grappled in the garden.

Luck was on Dietrich's side, however, and at last he managed to seize the Dwarf's belt and tear both it and his cape of invisibility from him. Deprived of his magical powers, the Dwarf-King was forced to submit to his conqueror.

As may be expected, by this victory Dietrich won the freedom of the Princess Simult but since, even in defeat, the Dwarf-King proved a treacherous enemy, Dietrich decided to bring him in chains to Verona and imprison him in a tower.

The Princess Simult went often to the tower to visit her one-time abductor. After a while, she realized that, indeed, she loved him well. And so, among much rejoicing and with the blessing of the magnanimous if somewhat bemused Dietrich, Laurin the Dwarf-King and the Princess Simult were wed.

Thereafter, the King of the Dwarfs and his beautiful Queen returned to the Tyrolean Mountains to rule in the valley of the Castle and to enjoy their Rose Garden. It is a beautiful and magical kingdom that, legend tells us, remains to this day. But it is a place that only the good and virtuous may ever discover.

THE AGE OF FANTASY

CASTLES IN FANTASTICAL LITERATURE

THE AGE OF FANTASY began with a brilliant flash of fire, a tremendous roar of thunder, and the evil smell of sulphur. It might have been the ancient satanic dragon once more on some vengeful vendetta against the Christian knights and their castle strongholds, but it was not.

In the real world, at least, a new alchemy was at work: gunpowder and cannon brought the great age of castles to an end. The walls collapsed before the new force, and feudal order with them. The security that castles once represented, the sense of permanence and order, melted away.

However, instead of disappearing from literature, the role of castles grew, if anything, more prominent. More than ever they became the centre of magical lands of fantasy and fairy-tale. Imaginary castles, the symbols of haven, became a necessary defence against the harsh reality of a new war technology that brought turmoil and social change in its wake, and on a massive scale. Imaginary castles were places of sanctuary and exotic adventure. Both the castles themselves and the adventures grew even more fanciful and extravagant now that they were no longer tied by the stones of a physical existence, or a pretence of a link to the real world.

This was an age of the highly literate and widely read story-teller steeped in ancient legends and the new-learned myths of the Orient. These educated men took pen in hand and to the old themes added rich new motifs and extraordinary and inventive new tales.

In the Renaissance, the themes of the old romances were revived. Often the old tales were made into elaborate contemporary allegories. In England the massive epic *The Faerie Queen*, based on Arthurian themes, was an allegory portraying an idealized court of Elizabeth I as Gloriana, the Faerie Queen.

However, perhaps the most delightful of all were the Italian comic allegories called *The Orlandos*. These tales were Italian reworkings of the romances of Charlemagne and his Palladins, particularly those relating to the great Roland – 'Orlando' to the Italians.

The view of Charlemagne's court is fantastic and fast paced. With ease its heroes make overnight trips to India and to the moon, between pursuing amorous adventures of extraordinary complexity.

The tales are chaotic and bombastic and filled with monsters and imaginary beasts, but there is an elegance and intelligence in the writing that is remarkable. Amidst the comedy and wit, there is also metaphysical depth combined with strikingly modern asides to the reader: as, for instance, when the plight of the heroes looks hopeless the narrator murmurs, 'Don't fret – they're only made of cardboard'.

With wit and humanity *The Orlandos* introduced new and sophisticated elements to the lore of castles.

TYPICALLY, THE ORLANDOS turn chivalric traditions upside-down for wonderfully amusing effect. One such adventure has a Maid-in-White-Armour on a quest to rescue her true love, a poor Knight-in-Distress held captive in the castle of a Wizard. The warrior-maid is the Christian Amazon Bradamant, sister to the Palladin Renaldo – the Italian Renaud of Montaubon.

THE CASTLES OF THE WIZARD
AND THE HIPPOGRIFF

THE CAPTIVE KNIGHT ROGERO, a true and valiant warrior, had wandered into the infinite mazes of the Castle of Atlas, an ancient and white-bearded magician who rode a winged steed called the Hippogriff – a beast part horse and part griffin.

To this vast mountain castle rode the warrior-maid Bradamant, bent on rescuing her lover. But Rogero had been trapped because he believed he heard Bradamant's voice within. He is destined to follow the phantom voice forever in the fantasy castle, for the infinite chambers of the labyrinth he was wandering in were the creation of his own mind, and, like many other of Atlas's prisoners, he cannot escape unless the spell is broken.

Bradamant, hearing Rogero's call, was herself drawn toward the castle entrance, and she, too, was about to be trapped by phantom voices into its dungeons.

However, in the nick of time, another of the Palladins, the brave Astolfo, arrived with a magic horn, the blast of which dispelled all fantasy. With one clarion call from the horn the Castle of the Wizard vanished into thin air. Rogero and many other prisoners found themselves sitting, blank and stunned, on lumps of rock all over the mountainside where once they believed a great castle stood.

THE CASTLE OF EARTHLY PARADISE

IN A MILD PARODY of the Grail Quest, the Palladin Astolfo, whose horn caused the phantom castle of Atlas to vanish, attempts the supreme test by capturing the Hippogriff and using it to fly to the ruby towers of the Castle of Earthly Paradise. His quest is to seek a cure for his friend Orlando's madness, in order that Charlemagne may have a full complement of Palladins to assist him in his coming battle against the Moors.

In the Earthly Paradise, Astolfo interviews many saints and apostles, but in order to find the solution to Orlando's madness, St. John takes him to that place of lunacy – the Moon! There in a valley he finds Orlando's lost senses and retrieves them. Before leaving the moon Astolfo is also shown a vision of the Fates weaving Destiny from the threads of the stream of Oblivion. The quest is successful, and Orlando's sanity is restored.

THE PALACE
OF OBLIVION

O RLANDO AND
FLORISMART, the Lord of the
Sylvan Tower, had been entrapped
in the Palace of Oblivion by a
maiden bearing a silver cup. It was her habit
to await travellers on the bridge which stood
by the palace and offer them a drink to quench
their thirst. Loath to refuse the offer, the
knights would drink and instantly forget the
purpose of their journey, their names and their
past lives. They were then confined to a
not-unpleasant life in the service of the damsel.

Astolfo, forewarned, rejected the cup and
dashed it to the ground, where it burst into
flames. He was then assaulted by numerous
knights, including many of his old friends,
who rushed to avenge the slight cast on their
mistress. It was left to the heroine, Angelica,
to rescue all the knights by using her magic
ring to dispel the enchantment.

Their memories restored, all the Palladins
rode on to new adventures.

OBERON

ONE of the most persistent figures in European legend is the supernatural Dwarf modelled on Andvari, the diminutive guardian of the gold horde and Ring of the Volsungs. In the German *Nibelungenlied* he is known as Alberich the Dwarf. In both he is a sinister figure, but in later romance his powers become changed, more varied, and he often lends assistance to various heroes under alternate names – Alberich, Alferich. In the tales of Dietrich he is Laurin, for Charlemagne he is Elbeghast.

But the transformation of character is truly striking once he becomes the English Auberon. By Shakespeare's time he had been converted into Oberon, the King of Faeries, a fantastic figure which the bard took as a major element in his *Midsummer Night's Dream*.

Oberon, the King of the Fairies, lives in a shimmering Castle of Gold in an enchanted forest not far from the shores of the Red Sea. Oberon is now considered to be the son of no less a personage than Julius Caesar and of Morgan Le Fay! He is described as being a radiant god of love who rides in a silver chariot drawn by leopards. He possesses a magical wand with the power to put all into a trance of sleep, and a magic goblet that gives eternal wine to the virtuous Christian but burns the lips of the sinner and infidel.

Oberon has his dark aspect, for he can command tempests, and the sound of his ivory horn causes people to dance frantically until they collapse in total exhaustion. At any rate, there is no doubt about his being a very powerful figure.

Among the many hero tales attached to Oberon is that of the Palladin, Huon of Bordeaux. Huon had been sent by an angry Charlemagne to the far kingdom of Babylon on a quest which all believed to be totally impossible. In his wanderings, however, Huon came across Oberon and his Castle of Gold in the enchanted forest. Oberon became Huon's protector, and the Palladin, with the help of the Faerie King, achieves his quest.

In Oberon's tales, however, even the Castles themselves take on a magical life of their own. This was the case when Huon attempted to win Oberon's Ring of Invincibility by entering the castle of the giant Angoulafre. The real challenge to Huon did not come from the Giant, whom Huon managed to slay in battle, but from the Castle itself. The structure literally has 'watchtowers' – towers that watch over the kingdom with magically animated eyes and warn the Giant of those who approach. Furthermore, the narrow drawbridge is guarded by giant mechanical bronze warriors armed with massive whirling flails.

Despite the obstacles of the fantastic castle, Huon wins the ring, and completes his quest in far Babylon. Finally, through Oberon's interventions – a brilliant guardian angel appearing and disappearing at will – Huon is reconciled with Charlemagne and reinstated in his court.

THE BLOODY CASTLE OF ALTARIPA

IN ANOTHER ADVENTURE, the hapless knight Rogero found himself once again immured in a castle. This was the Castle of Altaripa whose walls were stained with the blood of slain knights and whose parapets were decorated with their severed heads.

Rogero discovered the means by which they had been slain when he, too, was dropped into a pit within the keep, where a terrible monster attempted to devour him. Rogero at first stood firm to fight the creature, but soon discovered his weapons were useless against the beast's sword-proof hide. Prudently he leapt high up to a rafter out of the monster's grasp and remained there for some time while the beast vainly tried to reach him.

Now, to his chagrin, the Amazon Bradamant arrived. Rogero was too proud to be rescued yet again by the warrior-maid and refused her aid – preferring to stay there and die of starvation rather than be saved and die of embarrassment.

Before departing, Bradamant secretly dropped cakes of wax and a rope full of nooses into the pit. The beast gobbled up the cakes which cemented his terrible teeth in such a way that he could not open his mouth, and in his frenzied leaping about his feet soon became entangled in the looped rope so that he tripped up and collapsed.

Rogero quickly seized his opportunity and, leaping down from his beam, he grabbed the monster from behind as it lay on the ground and throttled it. He then escaped from the castle with the aid of a file, also left by Bradamant.

AMONG THE MANY HEROIC STORIES of Spain and Portugal, the most famous and characteristic are those concerning Amadis of Gaul and his descendants. Cervantes, the author of *Don Quixote*, knew and admired their fantastic mixture of the romances of Arthur and Charlemagne with a strong dose of Moorish mysticism, in settings ranging from Babylon and Constantinople to the Isles of Scotland. One of the numerous adventures of Amadis was the winning of the Castle of the Enchanter-King Apollidon.

AMADIS AND THE CASTLE OF APOLLIDON ON THE FIRM ISLAND

THE PALACE of the Enchanter-King Apollidon, called The Firm Island, was adorned with gemstones and fine wood; within were gardens which bloomed the year round. The Enchanter-King had left long since, but his spells preserved the place for the knight who would win his way through various trials to become the new heir of castle and kingdom.

The first test lay in the Arch of True Lovers. This was surmounted by a brazen statue holding a horn which belched smoke and flames at anyone who had been untrue in love, but blew sweet fragrances over those who had not. Amadis passed the Arch without mishap and went on to battle his way through an army of invisible assailants. He fought his way to his goal, the Forbidden Chamber, where he claimed the ancient throne of Apollidon. He was declared the new king and the spell over the land was broken.

ESPLANDIAN AND THE
FORBIDDEN MOUNTAIN

AMADIS HAD A SON, ESPLANDIAN, who inherited his father's courage. The youth took on the task of rescuing Lisuate, the King of Scotland, from the clutches of the enchanter-giant Archalaus who, with his monstrous family, had long waged war on mankind from his island fortress – The Forbidden Mountain.

Esplandian was assisted in this exploit by the fairy Urganda the Unknown, who carried him across the sea in her marvellous ship, the Green Serpent.

His benefactress deposited him on a rocky, serpent-strewn island, topped by the towering edifice of the giant's castle. Before climbing to the fortress itself, Esplandian first had to enter a marble vault by withdrawing the jewelled sword which held it shut, then slay a fierce dragon which guarded the place before claiming the scabbard which lay within.

Then, weapon in hand, the young man made his way up a narrow path towards the grim abode of Archalaus. This, too, was guarded by a gigantic sentinel, the son of Archalaus. He first scorned the youthful challenger, but at last fought and fell before Esplandian's flashing blade. The hero entered and defeated the rest of the family of wizards and finally, in a terrible duel, overthrew Archalaus himself.

Then Esplandian, together with the rescued king, was carried home by Urganda the Unknown.

IN THE FRENCH TALE OF LE BEL INCONNU, elements of older Arthurian stories – Gareth and Castle Perilous, Gawain and the Castle of Wonders and the Grail stories – are woven together in a glorious celebration of the art of story-telling.

The tale begins like that of Gareth, with a young man who makes his way to Arthur's court. He is unknown, and himself does not know his own name or that of his father. He becomes known as Le Bel Inconnu, the Fair Unknown.

LE BEL INCONNU
AND THE CASTLE OF SENAUDON

A YOUNG PRINCESS NAMED HELIE once came to Arthur's court to plead that he would send some great knight to rescue her mistress, Blonde Esmeree, the Queen of Wales, who had been transformed by the wizard Mabon into a dragon. She could be rescued only by a knight who could overcome many perils and enchantments, and then release her from the spell with a kiss.

Bound by a promise to the Fair Unknown, King Arthur had to send the untried youth. The princess was insulted by this turn of events, but reluctantly accepted his services. The way to Senaudon was fraught with peril, but the young knight proved a match for all the dangers that confronted them.

He overcame four powerful knights and two giants before they arrived at the Golden Island, which a terrible knight had besieged for five years. The causeway to the Island, lined with spikes decorated with the impaled heads of slain warriors, was gruesome testimony to the prowess of the knight. Undeterred, the Fair Unknown slew the Knight and crossed the causeway to the Golden Island on which stood a castle with crystal walls, seven black towers and a garden of magical trees, spices and flowers. This, however, was not the castle of the Blonde Esmeree, but of the lovely fay, La Pucelle aux Blanches Mains, the Maiden of the White Hands.

The Dark Knight of the causeway had held La Pucelle prisoner in her own castle because she refused to marry him, but now, she offered her love and her kingdom to her rescuer. The Fair Unknown, though enchanted by the beauty of La Pucelle, decided that he must remain true to his allegiance to Arthur and the quest he had embarked upon. With Princess Helie, he stole away from the Golden Island.

After a long and arduous journey they arrived at the Waste City, once magnificent, but now an abandoned ruin. The Fair Unknown rode alone through the broken gate, past crumbling towers and down deserted streets. At each broken window in the Queen's great castle there stood a ghostly minstrel with a lighted candle, calling welcome.

The Fair Unknown entered the hall. In the darkness a huge knight attacked him, but the young man drove him back. Next he heard a sinister whispering in the dark; this was revealed to be the whirling of magical axes cutting through the air towards him. With the greatest effort he managed to defend himself from their blows, only to be confronted once again by the huge knight, this time on the back of a powerful fire-breathing horse.

Hard pressed though he was, the Fair Unknown struck down the knight with a fatal blow. The knight proved to be the wizard Mabon, an evil Undead Being, and before the young man's eyes, the creature turned into a mass of rotten, maggot-infested flesh. At the same moment, the candles of the ghostly minstrels were all snuffed out, and the castle plunged into darkness as these spirits, too, fled the place.

But then the hall was lit by a fiery glow, emanating from a hideous fire-breathing dragon which entered. The Fair Unknown saw the jewelled eyes above the torch of the tongue as the serpent glided swiftly towards him. He bravely stood his ground and allowed himself to be kissed by the creature. Then he fell into a swoon in which he heard a mysterious voice naming him Guinglain, son of Gawain. Upon awakening, Guinglain discovered the hall full of light with the lovely Queen, Blonde Esmeree, now restored to her true form, by his side. The spell had been broken, the spirits had fled, and the city was once more beautiful and thronging with life.

Rejoicing in at last learning his true identity, Guinglain journeyed to Arthur's court to claim his heritage. But, in time, he returned to the kingdom he had restored to life and there married Blonde Esmeree. Together they ruled from their castle of Senaudon as King and Queen of Wales

CASTLES IN THE INFERNO

FANTASTIC TALES OF JOURNEYS into Hell-like castle kingdoms reached a highly systematized allegorical state in the popular English morality plays – *Pilgrim's Progress* probably being the most elaborate and complex. However, this was an extremely humble effort compared with the Italian masterwork *The Divine Comedy*, by Dante.

Dante's epic has many allegorical castles and towers, particularly in the Inferno, his version of Hell. There we find the greatest castle of all. This is the Castle of Dis (or Satan). As might be expected, everything in Hell is the reverse of things on earth.

The Castle of Dis is not on a mountain, but in a deep pit. Its walls are not to keep people out, but rather to hold souls in. The walls of the castle are moated by the river of death, the Styx. Its watchtowers are garrisoned by evil spirits and fallen angels. The single gate is guarded by Furies and Gorgons. Its walls are red hot and guard further rings of Hell that lead ever downward to a huge pit filled with all the terrible tortures of the soul. These are followed by even more rings of fortifications and finally the hot centre of the earth, where the dreadful chained spirit of Satan himself stands.

FAIRY TALE CASTLES

IN THAT VAST BODY OF FOLKLORE called Fairy Tales, the Castle is the centre of a kingdom of imagination where anything and everything is possible.

In the fairy tale the Castle is not allegorical, nor is it heavily Christian, except at times in terms of very basic morality. Primarily the Castle is symbolic of a walled world of imagination where magic works. It is a world where giants are overthrown, dragons slain and maidens rescued: a world where virtue and intelligence are rewarded. It is a world that fills a need in us all – a need to know that a timeless dreamland exists where our wishes are commands.

FAIRY TALES are by nature softer and gentler stories than the more violent, hot-blooded myths and legends from which they often spring. Certainly this is true of the Sleeping Princess tales that find an early expression in the violent Volsung Saga with Brynhild, the Valkyrie, who is put to sleep by a thorn in a tower surrounded by a wall of fire and of shields.

The most famous of the Sleeping Princess tales is that of Briar-Rose.

BRIAR-ROSE

THE LOVELY PRINCESS BRIAR-ROSE was cursed by a witch at her birth. The curse said that at fifteen, she would prick her finger on a spindle and fall into an enchanted sleep.

The king attempted to save his daughter by destroying all the spinning wheels in the kingdom, but his efforts proved futile for the princess discovered one in an abandoned tower and pricked her finger. Instantly the enchantment of sleep overtook her, and the whole castle. All about the neglected, sleeping castle an impenetrable wall of thorns quickly grew.

Many brave men attempted to rescue the Princess Briar-Rose, but they all became entrapped and died piteously amid the thorns. Exactly one hundred years had passed when a handsome young prince, hearing of the Sleeping Princess, approached the wall of thorns. Magically the thorn thicket parted of its own accord, and burst into huge, glowing flowers.

For this was the chosen prince, the only one who could walk unharmed into the sleeping castle and the tower of the princess. His kiss awoke her, and with her, the whole castle, from its century of slumber. The Prince and Briar-Rose declared they would be wed that very day.

THERE ARE MANY CASTLES of Sleeping Princesses in fairy tales, and in virtually all European countries. The Brothers Grimm recorded one particularly charming story of the princess asleep in a crystal coffin in a subterranean chamber under a mountain. At her side in the same chamber was a glass box which contained her magically miniaturized castles and kingdom. There she awaited the coming of the prince. An English variation on the theme is the tale of the Castle of Melvales.

THE CASTLE OF MELVALES

THE THREE SONS of the King of England once set out to find the magic apples which were the only cure for their father's illness. With the help of three mysterious old men, the youngest son eventually arrived at the Castle of Melvales.

He was instructed to cross the black moat surrounding the castle by summoning three swans which would carry him over. This done, he then had to pass by the sleeping forms of Giants, Dragons and Lions which lay before the gates, and thereafter find his way to the kitchen to steal the apples. All this had to be accomplished within the space of one hour, for if he were to be discovered in the castle when everyone awoke he would be turned into a monster himself.

On his way through the sleeping palace the boy passed the bedroom of a beautiful princess. He stopped to admire her, and kissed her before rushing on to complete his task. Eventually, after being cheated by his treacherous brothers, he was reinstated by the princess, who arrived with an army to claim him as her husband.

FREQUENTLY THE MAGICAL ENCHANTMENTS of fairy tale castles caused a metamorphosis in those who ventured in or near them. Most often people were transformed into birds or beasts, while less commonly they became trees or even stones. There were many variations on these castles, among them the Grimm tale of Jorinde and Joringel at the Castle of the Birds.

THE CASTLE OF THE BIRDS

ONCE A MAID AND A LAD named Jorinde and Joringel, who loved each other dearly, went for a walk in a mysterious wood. Soon they became quite lost and as they came to a clearing they looked up and saw the towers of an unknown castle. Suddenly Joringel found he could not move or speak, and though he was unharmed it seemed as if he had been turned to stone. Meanwhile Jorinde, on the contrary, found that she had never moved so fast in all her life, in fact, she now could fly – for she had been transformed into a nightingale!

For this was the spell of the castle in the wood. If travellers came too near, the men were turned into statues and the women tranformed into songbirds, and the witch who lived in the castle would appear in the form of an owl to capture the defenceless bird and take it into the castle.

This is exactly what happened to poor Jorinde, while the helpless Joringel was forced to look on. The next day, Joringel was freed from the spell, but knew he could not now approach the castle without being turned to stone once again. And though he wished nothing so much as to free his beloved Jorinde, he could not think of how to do this.

Then one night he dreamed of a magical blood-red flower with a large pearl at its centre. For nine days Joringel searched and at last he found a beautiful blood-red flower with a dew-drop the size of a pearl at its centre.

Armed with the flower, Joringel broke the enchantment of the castle and the old witch who lived there. The gates flew open at his touch and within he found not only the old crone, and his nightingale sweetheart, but seven thousand other birds in wicker cages. With a single touch of the red flower Jorinde was restored to her former state, and similarly – to the screams and curses of the witch – Joringel transformed the seven thousand songbirds back into the maidens they once had been.

IN MANY FAIRY TALES it is the occupant of the castle, and not the visitor, who is tranformed by a spell into an inhuman form. The classic example of this is the tale of Beauty and the Beast. In such tales the visitor comes to a castle haunted by the occupant in his or her beastly form, and by undergoing trials of strength or virtue or bravery manages to break the spell.

THE CASTLE OF THE CROW

ONCE A YOUNG PRINCESS ventured into the tangled but beautiful garden of a ruined castle and there discovered a badly torn and hurt crow caught in a rosebush. The crow had the gift of speech and told the Princess that he was in fact a Prince under a spell that only a brave princess might break.

The kind Princess, seeing that the crow was forced to endure torture as well as transformation, promised to do what she could. So that night she went as the crow had instructed her to the bedchamber in the ruined castle and slept in the great golden bed. She had been told she must remain there until dawn, and that no matter what the provocation she must not, on any account, cry out.

Dutifully the Princess did as she was told, but at the stroke of midnight a host of strange and monstrous beings burst into her room. Howling and screaming horribly the creatures grabbed the tight-lipped Princess and dragged her toward the fireplace where a huge cauldron boiled. But even though they pulled the girl to the very edge of the pot, and even though she was in fact terrified, the Princess did not cry out. Just then the cock crowed, announcing dawn, and the demons vanished.

The next day in the garden, the crow came to thank the Princess, for his suffering had already greatly diminished. But the Princess wished to do still more, so she came to the bedchamber each night for nearly three years, until at last, the crow became a handsome Prince he had once been and the ruined castle itself was returned to its former glory. And here the two were wed and happily lived and ruled their kingdom for one hundred years.

THE CASTLE OF THE SERPENT

A LITTLE SOLDIER ONCE CAME HOME from the wars, but on his journey chanced upon a deserted castle in a dark wood. When he entered the castle, he stood before the hearth to light his pipe. Suddenly out of the coals a serpent with a woman's head reared itself and swayed before him. Instead of fleeing, the brave little soldier stood to fight.

But the serpent spoke, and he became enchanted with her beautiful eyes and face. She was actually Ludovine, the daughter of the King, but she had been transformed by a malevolent enemy. To rescue her, the little soldier had to bring her three things from three rooms in the castle: her tunic, her skirt and her shoes.

When the little soldier entered the first room he found he must fight his way through a flock of disembodied fists to obtain the tunic, but this achieved, the Princess was transformed back to a woman as far as her waist.

Next the little soldier entered a room with eight arms holding sticks: the skirt he fought for transformed the Princess as far as her knees. Finally he battled his way through a room with eight goblins who had eyes of flame and were armed with powerful hammers. These, too, he overthrew and won the shoes that completed the Princess's transformation and totally broke the spell.

ANOTHER KIND of transformation occurs in the Scottish border ballad about the witch, Alison Gross, 'the ugliest witch in the north country'. A young lad is lured to her lonely tower and promised all sorts of riches and finery if he will be her lover. Her gifts are rejected, and in anger she takes out her silver wand, blows her grass-green horn and turns the hapless lad into a serpent, condemned to crawl eternally around an old tree. Fortunately the Queen of Faerie passes by one day, takes pity on the creature, breaks the spell and takes the restored youth to her own home.

ANOTHER VERY OLD SCOTTISH BALLAD is that of Childe Rowland. This has found various manifestations, not just in song and folk tale, but in Shakespeare's *King Lear* and Robert Browning's poem *Childe Rowland to the Dark Tower Came*. It is an eloquent expression of the fairy tale themes of capture and enchantment.

CHILDE ROWLAND AND BURD ELLEN

CHILDE ROWLAND'S FAIR SISTER, Burd Ellen, was once abducted by the King of Elfland. Childe Rowland searched out the Elf King's Dark Tower which was, in fact, a terrace-ringed fairy hill. By circling the Tower three times and using a secret command, Childe Rowland caused a great door to open in the hollow hill and entered the glittering twilight castle of the Elf King. This castle was built of spectacular rock crystal and gemstones, with high cathedral-like arches and an immense lamp, made of one giant pearl, hanging from a golden chain.

Here Childe Rowland found his sister, the fair Burd Ellen, and the King of Elfland. When traps of enchantment failed against Childe Rowland, the Elf King resorted to force. However, not even he could overthrow the stalwart youth, and the faerie found he must submit or die. The Elf King freed Burd Ellen from her enchantment, and she and her brother passed safely out of the Dark Tower, never to return again.

THERE SEEMS TO BE an almost infinite variety of castles in fairy tales from the absurd to the sublime. There are tales of castles of copper, iron, ebony, and glass: castles that float in the air and undersea castles made of shells. There are many tales of castles of crystal, one floating on a lake of quicksilver.

One story tells of a castle with twelve magic windows through which a princess can see into every corner of the world. Her suitors must play a deadly game of hide-and-seek with her, and the losers' heads are consigned to her battlements.

The Polish fairy tale called *The Glass Mountain* has a Castle of Gold with a captive princess on a mountain of pure glass. For years princes and heroes fall to their death while attempting the ascent. But in the seventh year a youth at last completes the climb by fastening bearclaws to his hands and feet.

CASTLES OF FAIRY TALE GIANTS

ONE OF THE MOST POPULAR THEMES in fairy tales is that of the giant's magical castle. The hero who dares to enter the giant's castle and slay him has his roots in the myths of Odin, Thor, Arthur, Dietrich and many other early figures. However, such tales as Jack-and-the-Beanstalk and Jack-the-Giant-Killer, which demonstrate the superiority of native cunning and quick-wittedness over brute strength, obviously have always found an attentive audience in children who, after all, are forced to live in an everyday world with their huge lumbering parents and other brutishly tall and strong adults.

JACK AND THE CASTLE OF GALIGANTUS

AFTER YEARS OF ADVENTURES, during which he had slain nearly all the Giants of England, Jack-the-Giant-Killer set out on a long journey. In time he came to a part of the country he had never before visited and knocked on a lonely cottage door.

There an old man greeted him and gave him food and a bed. From the old man Jack learned that the whole of the countryside was enslaved by a huge Giant called Galigantus who made his stronghold in an enchanted castle on the top of a high mountain.

Within the castle was a Princess who had been snatched by magic from her father's garden and taken up in a chariot drawn through the air by two fiery dragons. Once within the castle, she, like many other lords and ladies held captive there, was transformed into a beast. The Princess was now an elegant white hind.

The very next morning Jack rose early and set out to overthrow the Giant. Upon coming to the Castle of Galigantus, Jack took from his sack the weapons of his war on giants: his invisible coat, his cap of knowledge, and his shoes of swiftness. So dressed, Jack began to climb the mountain to the castle and soon came to the gate. This was guarded by two fiery Griffins, but as he was wearing his coat of invisibility he boldly marched between the two monsters without concern.

He then climbed the castle's huge steps until at last he came to a massive bronze door from which hung a golden trumpet on a chain of fine silver. Under the horn was engraved the verse:

> Whoever shall this trumpet blow,
> Shall soon the Giant overthrow;
> And break the black Inchantment strait.
> So shall all be in happy State.

Jack quickly took the huge trumpet from the door and placing it to his lips blew as hard as he could. The blast of the trumpet was accompanied by a tremendous roar and a crash like a thunderstorm and an earthquake combined. The foundations of the castle rocked and split. Then came a great whirlwind that sucked up the debris of the ruin, the Giant, the Griffins and all the other evil inhabitants into the air.

But the Princess and all the lords and ladies were brought back to their human forms, freed at last from the tyranny of Galigantus.

173

CASTLES IN MODERN FANTASY

THE CASTLE IN MODERN FANTASY really began in the 18th century
with the first 'gothic novel', Sir Horace Walpole's *The Castle of Otranto*. At
the centre of the gothic novel was the great brooding castle haunted by an
avenging ghost or spirit. After the advent of the gothic
novel, the mere mention of a castle evoked an atmosphere
of horror, suspense, and an expectation of the macabre.
The early 19th century romantics seemed bewitched
by the spell of fantastic castles. Major figures of
literature, from Goethe and Jane Austen to Byron
and Keats, explored their haunted corridors and
dungeons. When it came to the first historical
novels of Sir Walter Scott – from *Ivanhoe* to his
last novel, *Castle Dangerous* – the castle had become
an essential element in fantastic fiction: as indeed in
the first science fiction novel, Mary Shelley's
unforgettable *Frankenstein*.

FOR MANY, however, the ultimate
haunting spirit of the castle was
conjured up in Bram Stoker's
late 19th century novel, *Dracula*.
In the distant, but real, mountains of
Transylvania, Stoker's hero travels
to the ancient Castle Dracula.
It is massive, a walled and turreted
edifice with a drawbridge, a great keep
and labyrinthine cellars and dungeons.

Count Dracula is the immortal
'undead' spirit of the castle, a modern
Satan, who may walk as a man only in
darkness. But he is a vampire who
prefers to transform himself into a large
bat so that he may crawl down the walls
of his castle and fly to the side of his
innocent sleeping victims to silently
drink their blood.

In Transylvania Count Dracula's reign of terror is absolute, but, like Satan, who attempted to enlarge his domain of the damned by entering Paradise, Dracula plans to extend his dominion. The rather gentlemanly Victorian Count of Darkness has decided to pack his coffins and depart from the safety of his kingdom to attempt no less than the eventual conquest of England.

It emerges, however, that Dracula's immortality and supernatural powers are limited by several factors. Being a pagan spirit, he fears the sign of the Cross. He cannot tolerate the light of day. And finally, if his body can be discovered undefended in its coffin bed, the Count can actually be killed if a stake is driven through his heart.

Once these facts are discovered, the potential victims of Count Dracula become vampire hunters. They track down the evil Count in his coffin in the crypt of his English castle, Carfax Abbey. There, moments before he is due to wake from his death sleep, a stake is driven through his heart, and his evil existence is put to an end.

IN COUNT DRACULA, Bram Stoker touched a chord deep in the human psyche, a nightmare vision that was both general and individual. Interestingly, Stoker's Dracula was based on a real Transylvanian Count Dracula of the 15th century, whose activities made the fictional Count look mildly eccentric.

The awesome cruelty and psychopathic behaviour of the real-life Count Dracula was a legend in his own time. On St. Bartholomew's Day 1460, he had 30,000 Romanian men, women and children impaled on stakes before his castle. On another occasion he had 20,000 Turks and Saxons impaled, and then held a picnic in a clearing in this torturer's forest of stakes for his terrified 'loyal' vassals.

The degree of Count Dracula's sadism was as astonishing as it was horrific. There are accounts of his having victims boiled, skinned and roasted alive. Some were forced to eat their own children before being killed, while others were simply torn to pieces and devoured by wild animals.

Impalement, however, remained Count Dracula's favourite method of killing, and it is estimated he disposed of some 100,000 people in this terrible manner. It is easy, therefore, to see how the idea of impaling Dracula might be an appropriate means of killing the most vicious impaler of all time.

ALTHOUGH DRACULA, whose name means both 'Devil' and 'Dragon', was certainly a bloodthirsty tyrant, there is no evidence of vampirism being directly linked with him. The element of vampirism very likely comes from much older practices of witchcraft and lycanthropy to which the image of a vampire bat-spirit inhabiting the old castle of Dracula seemed appropriate enough.

However, the taking of blood as a means of rejuvenating life is possibly a motif taken from another historic castle dweller in Transylvania. This was the notorious Elizabeth Bathory, who later became known as the Blood Countess.

Born to Transylvania's oldest noble family in the 16th century, she lived in the high mountain Castle Csejthe on the edge of Carpathia. She was a woman renowned for her beauty, which she boasted she could magically maintain forever. When at last the source of her personal fountain of youth was revealed, the hunt for the bodies of her victims was undertaken. At least fifty young girls had been kidnapped, tortured, murdered and had their blood drained from them. It transpired that the countess was literally bathing in the blood of maidens, in the belief that it revived her youth.

In 1611, a council of noblemen met and condemned the Countess's henchmen to death, and the Blood Countess herself was walled up in her own castle tower.

POE AND THE HOUSE OF USHER

O F ALL THE 19TH CENTURY WRITERS, it was Edgar Allan Poe who most clearly brought to life the concept that the gothic castle's atmosphere of terror was not so much an exotic setting in some fantastic realm, but was rather the image of a state of mind, a psychological insight into human terror, guilt and obsession.

Probably most vividly in his short story, *The Fall of the House of Usher*, Poe takes the elements of the gothic tale and compresses them into a black gem of literature, deeply insightful of human obsession with the macabre. The fall of the House of Usher becomes a metaphor for the disintegration of the human mind.

Filled with a terrible foreboding, the narrator arrives at the House of Usher, a decaying mansion with grey walls and turrets rising in the midst of a tarn, a deep black water pond. He rides over a causeway to the gate of the House and enters a gothic hall through dark and intricate passages.

This is the traditional home of the cursed aristocratic Usher family, of which only two remain – Roderick Usher and his fatally ill sister, Madeline. The place itself seems to be linked to the physical and mental collapse of the family. And although described as a 'House' the structure is built upon the foundations of a mediaeval castle, its dungeons and family crypt still intact.

The sense of dread is heightened by tales within the tale, one a poem of a haunted castle, the other a mythical story of a hero called Ethelred who enters a castle of gold with a floor of silver and is confronted by a dragon.

When, in due course, Madeline Usher is laid by Roderick and the unnamed narrator in her tomb, it emerges that she is not actually dead. At a critical moment, she arises from her premature burial, bloody and quite mad from tearing herself out of her own grave. Murderously she attacks her own brother. Horror-struck, the narrator flees across the causeway and as he does so the ghastly house shatters and, along with its demented inhabitants, is consumed with roaring violence by the black waters.

POE AND THE CASTLE
OF THE RED DEATH

IN 'THE MASQUE OF THE RED DEATH' Poe reverts to mediaeval times and the mediaeval allegory of the castle. It is a tale richly gothic in atmosphere, while retaining the stark simplicity of true allegory.

The principle character is the wealthy Prince Prospero, whose dominions have been ravaged by a plague called the Red Death. Rather than doing what he can for the terrible suffering of his people he retreats to one of his homes, a castellated Abbey, with a thousand of his favourite courtiers and ladies. His fortress is high-walled and impenetrable, and by the prince's orders the great gates are welded shut. The external world can take care of itself. There the plague may rage but within the Prince determines there will be gaiety and bounty. Rich provisions have been made, musicians, actors, exotic fare are all provided.

After five or six months of seclusion the Prince gives orders for a masked ball to be held in the great apartments which have been built to his bizarre and decadent tastes. These consist of seven great rooms, each with a large gothic window of stained glass lit by a brazier on a tripod which illuminates each room through the window. Each of the seven rooms has a different colour, and that colour is matched by the colour of the stained glass. However, the seventh room is draped in black velvet, contains a huge chiming ebony clock, and has a ruby red window – blood red.

In the midst of the grotesque masquerade, at the midnight chiming of the great clock, a masked figure appears which even among the fantastically costumed guests evokes a certain horror. The gaunt figure is like a corpse, wrapped in winding sheets dabbled with blood, the terrible mask on the face contorted and blotched like one who has perished by the Red Death. This costume, representing the real terror that Prince Prospero had deliberately shut out beyond his gates, is more than he can endure. Enraged, he orders the guest to be unmasked.

Pursuing the macabre figure to the velvet room, the Prince draws his dagger but, in the very shadow of the strange guest and of the ebony clock, Prospero collapses in death. Others leap upon the masked figure, tearing the mask from its face only to find to their horror that there is nothing there. The being is bodiless, as the Red Death is bodiless. And one by one the revellers themselves collapse in death. None of the thousand live. The castle that was to have been their salvation, becomes, instead, their sealed tomb.

KAFKA'S CASTLE

IN THE 20TH CENTURY, Franz Kafka, like Poe, took up the mediaeval allegory of the castle that had so much in common with the morality play of six centuries before.

Kafka, again like Poe, was one of the most deeply influential figures of his century. He saw a world of tortured creatures who seemed to exist only through their obsessions. His novel, *The Castle*, is usually interpreted as being an allegory of man's effort to seek out and know divinity.

The plot involves a man called K. who arrives on foot at a town dominated by a mysterious and immense castle. He has been summoned there, yet is continually turned away. Although it is admitted that he is expected, he can never find any figure of authority to grant him entrance. Every effort to learn why he has been sent for, or how he may gain an audience or learn who the inhabitants of the castle are, is frustrated.

Kafka's castle is a failed Grail legend. However, the unknowable divinity of the castle seems to be not a brilliant revelatory bringer of light, but a sinister, dark, bureaucratic head of a labyrinthine state: a divinity purposely frustrating and devious. The castle is a symbol of the state, the government. It is the structure and system symbolic of oppression and the mindless imposition of authority. It defends itself, demands of its vassals, and explains nothing.

K. does not know whether he has been summoned by Satan or by God. There is no evidence in fact that any master of the castle actually exists. The structure might conceivably have no one at all at its centre, in which case all the machinery of autocratic control functions as an ultimate black joke. And the final, appropriate frustration is that Kafka left the novel unfinished.

T. H. WHITE'S CAMELOT

IT SEEMS that the towers of Camelot must be rebuilt at least every century or so by a major figure in literature. The concept of the ideal kingdom changes, and therefore Camelot must be reshaped.

This was true of Malory's Camelot in *Morte d'Arthur*, Spencer's Elizabethan Camelot in the *Faerie Queene*, and the highly moral Victorian Camelot of Alfred Lord Tennyson in his *Idylls of the King*.

In the 20th century, T. H. White remade Camelot so that it would be habitable for the contemporary reader. In his *Once and Future King*, White created an Arthurian castle-kingdom filled with humour and humanity. His characters are warm, knowable, fallible, and highly personal, the antithesis of the stylized romantic knight. For the most part they seem to be ordinary people of basic decency, driven to great deeds by extraordinary circumstances. And in this they bear a close resemblance to Tolkien's hobbits – ordinary, comfortable creatures, often afraid, never daunted. Tolkien's Middle Earth and White's Camelot are built on one fundamental concept that simply says, 'Fight only for the good' – a concept that Arthur himself concluded had come too soon to his world, but whose time would come again. White's implication, of course, is that the time is now – the values that Camelot stood for are most urgently needed in our time.

THE LORD OF THE RINGS

THE MOST COMPLEX, fully realized and extensive invented world of castle-kingdoms in modern fantasy is certainly that of J.R.R. Tolkien in his monumental *Lord of the Rings* trilogy.

Tolkien's world of Middle-Earth was created by an imagination fueled by a massive knowledge of mythologies and literatures of the castle-kingdoms of Europe. Although Tolkien himself denied any allegorical intention in his work, his theme is that most ancient struggle, probably never to be resolved, between the powers of good and of evil.

In the wide lands of Middle-Earth, the kingdoms of Elves, Dwarves, and Men are at war with the dreadful forces of Sauron, the Dark Lord of Mordor. The centre and source of power in the mountain-ringed land of Mordor is the huge castle called Barad-Dûr, the Dark Tower of Sauron. From this tower Sauron commands his legions of goblin soldiers – the Orcs – and his armies of damned spirits of barbarian men.

Against this sea of darkness, only one realm stands fast, the castle-kingdom of Minas Tirith, the White Tower of Gondor. It is here, before the walls of the White Tower, that the greatest battle would rage, and the tide of war be turned against the Dark Lord.

However, it is only when the Dark Tower itself is toppled and entirely obliterated that the War of the Ring could be ended. Only then would the White Tower become the centre of a new world of peace and prosperity, a monument to all that is good and great in the world.

BARAD-DÛR

The Dark Tower of
Mordor

MINAS TIRITH

CITADEL
OF THE MEN OF GONDOR

GORMENGHAST

ALTHOUGH Tolkien's *The Lord of the Rings* has proved to be the most popular fantasy of the twentieth century, there is one other epic work that, for its own good reasons, more extensively explores and expands on the concept of the castle.

This is Mervyn Peake's astonishing creation, *Gormenghast*, an invented world not simply dominated by a castle but in which, essentially, the entire world is the castle, and in many respects the castle itself is the real subject of the fantasy.

Peake was primarily an artist but he was also a talented writer. Hence his visualization of the massive castle-city that is Gormenghast is graphic, vivid and as exact as any such vast and ancient sprawl of stone could be. For it is a truly stupendous series of structures, the whole edifice covering possibly hundreds of acres, its huge and ponderous halls, courtyards, terraces, wings, towers, flying buttresses and roofs representing generations of iconoclastic building throughout the history of the House of Groan.

Much of Gormenghast has been abandoned and has fallen into near ruin. Most is simply empty. The buildings still occupied, however, are extensive, their chambers cavernous, their corridors wide and long enough to permit young Titus Groan to ride them on his pony. Some of the buildings climb twelve storeys: many are covered with lichen, seeping moss and monstrous growths of ivy. The inhabitants are weird and grotesque, burdened with mindless custom but retaining that antic eccentricity peculiar to centuries of ingrown existence.

Actually, as a castle, Gormenghast seems to have no reason for being, for physical defence is unnecessary. But the real dangers are implicit in its mouldering walls. Indeed, the halls of Gormenghast echo with the shadows of Poe and Kafka, the weight of crumbling stone and meaningless ritual a marvellous external symbol of the convoluted rot within. Yet the larger-than-life characters, who might be caricatures were it not for their Dickensian richness, are by turns poignant, tender, vicious, droll, wildly ambitious, selflessly loyal, gross, occasionally uproariously funny – and always heartbreakingly real. Something in these burdened people speaks to us all. The reluctant inheritor of Gormenghast, the strange young anti-hero Titus Groan, in some respects might be viewed as a twentieth century Everyman. In Titus's struggle to free himself from the suffocating ruin of a castle with all its hidebound traditions and customs there is an echo of the modern day battle to cope with an accumulation of expectations that both threaten nightmare and promise millenium: something at once monumentally magnificent and hugely monstrous – both curse and gift.

Like the concept of the castle, *Gormenghast*, as a work of art, is extraordinary. And like the castle, it has many levels – as pure adventure, as a tale to be told, as an allegory of man's deathless struggle for freedom of the spirit, and finally as a masterwork, in and of itself, of staggering ingenuity and consummate artistry.

So, WELL INTO THE TWENTIETH CENTURY, THE
CREATORS OF DREAMS ARE FINDING NEW
MEANINGS IN OLD FORMS: THE ALLEGORY STILL
EXPANDS, ITS FORM MUTABLE, CHANGING TO FIT
OUR NEEDS, THE POWERFUL CENTRAL CONCEPT REMAINING
STEADFAST.

THE CASTLE, AND ALL IT REPRESENTS, WILL ALWAYS BE
WITH US. ONCE IT WAS BORN, ONCE THE STONE WAS MADE
LIVING, THE REPOSITORY OF POWER MADE REAL, THE IDEA
COULD NEVER BE UNMADE. EVEN IF ALL THE CASTLES OF THE
WORLD WERE DESTROYED, IN THE MINDS OF MEN THEY
WOULD BE BUILT ANEW; THE WIZARD CALLED IMAGINATION
WOULD RAISE HIGH WALLS AND TOWERS OUT OF RUINS

BIBLIOGRAPHY

The Earliest English Poems tr. M. Alexander   Penguin 1966

Beowulf tr. David Wright   Penguin 1957

H.A. Guerber *Myths of the Norsemen*   Harrap 1908

Charles Squire *Celtic Myth & Legend*   Gresham 1910

The Mabinogion tr. G. Jones & T. Jones   Dent 1949

A Celtic Miscellany tr. K. H. Jackson   Penguin 1971

Jean Markale *Women of the Celts*   Gordon Cremonesi 1975

Geoffrey de Monmouth *History of the Kings of Britain*   Penguin 1966

Chretien de Troyes *Arthurian Romances*   Dent 1967

Wolfram von Eschenbach *Parzival* tr. Helen M. Mustard and Charles E. Passage
    Vintage 1961

Sir Thomas Malory *Le Morte d'Arthur* ed. A.W. Pollard   Medici Society 1929

Richard Barber *The Arthurian Legends*   Boydell Press 1979

Richard Cavendish *King Arthur & the Grail*   Granada 1980

The Quest of the Holy Grail tr. P.M. Matarasso   Penguin 1969

Donald A. Mackenzie *Teutonic Myth and Legend*   Gresham 1910

A.R. Hope-Moncrief *Romance and Legend of Chivalry*   Gresham 1910

Ludovico Ariosto *Orlando Furioso*   Oxford University Press 1983

Dante *The Divine Comedy* tr. the Rev. Francis Cary   reprinted Omega 1982

Joseph Jacobs *More English Fairy Tales*   Nuft 1895

Andrew Lang *The Colored Fairy Books*   reprinted Dover 196-

Jacob & Wilhelm Grimm *Selected Tales* tr. David Luke   Penguin 1982

Iona & Peter Opie *The Classic Fairy Tales*   Oxford University Press 1974

Edgar Allen Poe *Tales of Mystery and Imagination*   reprinted Minerva 1971

Bram Stoker *Dracula*   Bantam 1981

Franz Kafka *The Castle*   Vintage 1974

J.R.R. Tolkien *The Lord of the Rings*   Allen & Unwin 1966

Mervyn Peake *The Gormenghast Trilogy*   Penguin 1969